THE ART OF

Being a Woman

THE ART OF

Being a Woman

a simple guide to everyday love and laughter

Véronique Vienne

with illustrations by Ward Schumaker

Clarkson Potter/Publishers
New York

Library of Congress
Cataloging-in-Publication Data
Vienne, Véronique.
The art of being a woman : a simple guide
to everyday love and laughter /
Véronique Vienne.
1. Quality of life—United States.
2. Happiness—United States. I. Title.
BF637.C5V53 2006
158—dc22   2006004597

ISBN-13: 978-0-307-33724-5
ISBN-10: 0-307-33724-3

Printed in the United States of America

Design by Maggie Hinders

10 9 8 7 6 5 4 3 2 1

First Edition

To all my American girlfriends,

who, without exception,

have been such great teachers.

acknowledgments

I always knew that I would ask Ward Schumaker to illustrate this book because he is the kind of man who looks at women with a mixture of admiration and disbelief—as I often do. Our collaboration gave us a precious opportunity to explore the commonality of our views. The only man involved in a project conceived for women and by women (the very supportive team at Clarkson Potter is all female), he often made us chuckle with his witty interpretation of feminine beauty.

Among the many women who helped me is first and foremost my agent, Helen Forson Pratt, a savvy critic and faithful supporter. This book also marks my ten-year association with the people at Clarkson Potter, some of whom I know well, others who work behind the scenes, but all trusted allies: Lauren Shakely, Pam Krauss, Doris Cooper, Elissa Altman, Marysarah Quinn, Maggie Hinders, Sibylle Kazeroid, and Alison Forner.

I also want to acknowledge here the friends and family members who gave me affectionate feedback: my husband, Bill Young; my daughter, Jeanne Lipsey; and kindred spirits Peggy Roalf, Nancy Cohen, and Phyllis Cox.

contents

W E women are the providers of joy. We can, with our very presence, brighten up the day. Just watch us approach a group of strangers—in a restaurant, a bus, or an elevator. If we feel good, within seconds everyone around us feels a little better. Our lightheartedness is contagious. With a glance, we can make men stand straighter; with a smile, we can help other women breathe easier. The art of being a woman is the art of lifting the spirits of others.

Indeed, because we are traditionally the life-givers (not only do we bring babies into the world, we are also the designated nurturers of all who need care), the task of reminding people that they are lucky to be alive falls on us.

Frankly, there are worse predicaments. All things considered, there is nothing wrong with being the one who makes a child beam, a friend laugh, or a fellow happy. The trick is to do so effortlessly, with no motive other than to have a good time.

As crummy as it seems now and then, life on planet Earth is full of wonderful surprises, not the least of them the fact that women by and large are such amazing people—tough, brave, generous, good-looking. And you—yes, *you*—happen to be one of them! This simple realization is all you need to feel the particular kind of joy the French call "joie de vivre"—joy of life.

It is the joy of being born a woman; it is the joy of knowing what it means to love; it is the joy of having the gift of laughter.

It all comes down to admitting that you are fortunate to be who you are. You could not trust anyone else to be inside your head, could you? Who else is likely to have your zany sense of humor, your uncanny ability to spot the next trend, your flexibility of mind, your talent for dating the wrong guy, and your endless compassion for old dogs?

Most of us do not appreciate enough the qualities we have. We practice self-deprecation as if it were a virtue. But to quote Nelson Mandela: "Your playing small does not serve the world. There is nothing enlightened about shrinking so that other people won't feel insecure." Take his word for it, and let your own light shine!

Being glad to be a woman is an art. To get the hang of it, you have to be willing to get rid of your self-doubts and acknowledge your innate gifts and talents. This book is written to do exactly that: to convince you to cherish your life and embrace the joy that is your birthright.

As a Frenchwoman who has lived most of her adult life in America, I had the advantage of being able to combine joie de vivre with the pursuit of happiness—a heady combo. In this simple guide to everyday love and laughter, I hope that you will find, as I did, the best of both worlds.

• •

·1·

You
(A SHORT EXHORTATION)

Y O U make a spirited, life-affirming statement when you do not apologize for being who you are. Indeed, to watch a woman take hold of a situation is a treat, her display of perspicacity the kind of joyful spectacle that makes one feel that there is hope for humanity, after all.

When you play it safe, though, the universe becomes a little duller.

The role of the mind in securing happiness is often underestimated. In America, we are more gratified by our accomplishments than by our ideas. However, for you and me, there are better uses for our mental dexterity than doing crossword puzzles. Downplaying our intelligence is cheating ourselves of one of the finest forms of gratification legally available: that of being a freethinking individual.

The French, in contrast, derive great pleasure from figuring things out, their Cartesian approach the source of endless satisfaction to them. Even though their famous joie de vivre is an emotion, as far as they are concerned, its origin is in the brain. It is a brief, unexpected thrill, as when you chuckle because you get the full impact of a joke, or you are tickled pink because you grasp the elegant absurdity of a paradox.

Descartes should have said: "I think, therefore I feel alive!"

Too many of us are afraid to deal with the fact that we can run circles around the other half of the world. Warned by Dorothy Parker that "men seldom make passes / at girls who wear glasses," we will strategically undermine our intelligence in public in order not to overpower or intimidate our entourage.

Flirtatiousness is no substitute for mental acuity. The

Use your head, and your heart will follow.

high-pitched voice, the reluctance to make eye contact, the restless body language, the pursed lips, the playing with your hair, the tossing aside of the long mane? It fools no one. A woman is most impressive when she puts aside her intellectual modesty and self-deprecating mannerisms and struts her stuff in broad daylight.

That woman is you when you decide to speak up at a meeting and the words that come out of your mouth are astute, earnest, and persuasive.

She is you when you pass a big rig on a long stretch of highway—pedal to the metal, elbow in the wind, clear-headed, your gaze locked on the horizon.

She is you when you explain to your dad how to order plane tickets online and at the end of the conversation he says, "I love you."

And she is you when you face your image in the mirror in the morning, a look of tacit connivance in your eyes, your mascara raised in the air as if you were about to make a toast.

So use your head, and your heart will follow.

• •

·2·

other women

(A SELF-ESTEEM PRIMER)

B E T W E E N women, a lot of silent admiration passes back and forth, each furtive glance reinforcing the sense of specialness that makes us who we are. All day long, in what can best be described as a voracious lovefest, we observe each other ceaselessly, noting every subliminal fashion detail, absorbing countless tips about hair and makeup, and evaluating every wardrobe do and don't with a connoisseur's eye.

What some of us might experience as female competitiveness is in fact an ongoing learning process. Calling it jealousy or envy is a misnomer. Granted, women often seem rapacious in their quest for the sort of information that might alleviate some gnawing hunger in their psyche. But the motive that drives them as they scrutinize the coded data embedded in the other person's physical appearance is essentially a subconscious desire for self-knowledge, not a primordial urge to outdo potential rivals and eliminate them.

In fact, it does not take much—only a small mind shift—to see other women as the teachers they really are instead of the fierce competitors they are sometimes portrayed to be. You can forever change the way you think about other women by systematically seeking the company of members of the fair sex over a short period of time and actively challenging the assumption that their many qualities are a threat to your ego.

Make it a week of pampering and indulging if you must. Stop by the local nail salon for a manicure and see if you can get a shampoo and blow-dry at your hairstylist's. Go explore the latest shopping district. Lose yourself among the stalls at an outdoor crafts fair. Clock some treadmill time at a busy health club, or, if you are not in a spandex mood, hang out at a bar during happy hour.

Watch how quickly and efficiently you absorb lessons from your unwitting mentors. This woman holds her head with regal assurance? That one steps out of a taxi with the stealth of a cat? And yet another one could melt an iceberg with her girlish smile? Enjoy it all, as if each pleasing characteristic you observe in other women were an encrypted message to be deciphered and used to develop your own aptitudes and talents.

> Think of female jealousy as feminine curiosity, as an impulsive desire to learn as many things as possible.

Thinking of other women as a source of inspiration is surprisingly satisfying—and practical to boot. To draw from the communal reservoir of knowledge women share between them, all you need to do is get out of the house. Sit at a busy coffee-shop counter and order a bowl of soup, wait in line at the post office, or stroll through a playground among the moms and the nannies. There you will find them, in all their protean femininity! Each woman a paragon, each one exemplary in her own inimitable way.

People watching, a popular pastime everywhere, is more than simply entertainment. By reinforcing a sense of community, it brings out the performer in all of us. In cafés, restaurants, marketplaces, parks, or stadiums, men and women alike exhibit their favorite personae in front of an audience of keen observers whose approval—or disapproval—we all seek.

But the qualities we admire in women, unlike the qualities we admire in men, do not have to be spectacular in order to be personable. Blond bombshells notwithstanding, the woman who really appeals to you in a crowded room is probably not the prettiest or the best dressed, but someone oddly graceful whose demeanor somehow piques your curiosity.

Appreciating hidden virtues in other women will teach you to value your own qualities, not the least of them your ability to spot greatness in ordinary folks. What better way to boost your self-esteem than to trust your own discernment? You know that growing up female is no small deed, so hail the courage, hard work, and grit of any woman who has lived long enough to become a decent human being.

It takes one to know one—it takes a great woman to spot greatness in other women. Every time you notice something you like in another woman, you can rest assured that the same quality exists in you.

In fact, why not assume that, at any given moment, your intrinsic worth is equal to the sum total of the qualities you have openly admired in other women during the last twelve hours?

The gratitude we feel when we acclaim others is one of the most confounding mysteries of the human heart.

Why is it so much fun to give a performer a standing ovation? Did you ever envy the people who throw bouquets at a diva taking her bow on the stage? And don't you love to clap at the end of a colleague's stellar business presentation? Most of us would hate to miss an opportunity to jump on a bandwagon. Curiously, congratulating someone we admire comforts the soul.

As the French moralist La Rochefoucauld remarked centuries ago: "We would not experience as much pleasure in life if we held back compliments."

So far, in our culture, men enjoy a near exclusivity when it comes to complimenting women (not counting the now-standard "you look fabulous today" formula, a popular greeting among girlfriends). Why do men get all the glory and most of the psychological benefits from commending women on their achievements as well as their beauty? There is no valid reason why you and I cannot do the same and buck up our own egos by telling a woman friend, a colleague, a niece, or a sister-in-law what an amazing person she is to us.

I am not suggesting you wax poetic about her appearance. Look beyond the facade. You could tell her, for instance, that you wish you were half as smart as she is when it comes to politics, real estate, and money management.

If you are in an expansive mood, laud in the same breath her fashion flair, her negotiating skills, and her amazing kindness. Or pull out all the stops and praise recklessly her discernment, cleverness, math ability, leadership qualities, winning personality, and adorable freckles.

The greatness you celebrate in all women
(not just in some of them) is the very quality
that makes you great.

As compelling as it is, the concept of sisterhood falls short of acknowledging the fact that all women, regardless of their circumstances, have something unique to share with others. *Sisterhood* is not inclusive enough, the word suggesting a club rather than a species, a clan instead of a tribe. It doesn't do justice to the vast network of firing neurons that links your son's babysitter to his matronly school-bus driver, and the pregnant grocery-store cashier to her second husband's first wife.

*Imagine her capable of
some awe-inspiring act of bravery.*

Striving to find qualities to celebrate in every woman, whether she is the bedraggled mother of triplets or the prim and proper flight attendant, is the occasion for you to stretch your imagination. Uncover that specific je ne sais quoi that makes her a likable human being and feel how more likable *you* become as a result. Your self-esteem gets a shot in the arm as you take note of her big brown eyes as bright as lanterns, or her handsome, tired features softened by years of caring for others.

So, instead of wasting valuable energy wondering whether a particular woman deserves your praises, assume that she is someone whose life story could very well be an amazing tale of courage and altruism. Take a second look and imagine her capable of some awe-inspiring act of bravery.

> You never know: the woman sitting next to you could harbor the most amazing soul.

Remember this the next time you are tempted to criticize the way a mother spoils her child, for instance. Lighten up if you catch yourself staring disapprovingly at a teenage girl who is exhibiting her tattooed midriff. And don't begrudge the woman in your yoga class who flaunts the fact that she can twist herself into a pretzel. Give all women the thumbs-up (even the pushy cosmetics-counter attendant with the sugar-coated voice). Make no exception. Become the self-designated champion of all unsung female heroes.

friendship

(WORDS OF ENCOURAGEMENT)

THESE days, girlfriends are giving each other permission to get older. Permission to get older? You bet. Permission to have gray hair, laugh lines—and a fabulous figure.

And while we are on the topic of permissions granted by women to women, add the permission to live and learn, take

*The perception that women are feeble creatures
is pure mythology.*

a lover, stay home with the kids and still hire a nanny, go
frizzy, call in sick, cry a river, cancel a lunch date at the last
minute because something better came up, spend next
month's rent on a weekend at Canyon Ranch, bite the bul-

let, upgrade to business class, make whoopee, ask him to marry you, sue the bastard, and believe that a year from now you will be able to fit into the dress you wore on your graduation day.

At all times, women give each other encouraging go-aheads. A glance, a smile, a silence, or a second of hesitation can be interpreted as a sign of approval. We root for each other even as we seem to disapprove. Whether we hate a friend's haircut or wish she'd stop complaining about her job, we are expressing a desire for her to lead a happier life.

There is some compelling scientific evidence that societies in which women are happier tend to be healthier overall. Men in particular live longer. Furthermore, equality between the sexes is also a positive health factor. Statistically speaking, strong women who have a high status keep illnesses at bay in their communities.

So, whether or not they know it, when women encourage each other to claim happiness as their birthright, they do so for the benefit of all.

> Let's be here for each other: it is in our self-interest to contribute to the cheerfulness of all our women friends.

These days, who wants to be cast as a member of the weaker sex? The perception that women are feeble creatures is pure mythology. In fact, we are learning every day to reinterpret our so-called frailties as strengths. We see true grit where others might see only stubbornness; we call tenacity what a husband might endure as intractability; we admire a friend's recklessness even though her accountant often wishes she'd be more risk adverse.

We turn to each other for advice (and are seldom disappointed in that regard), but truth be told, what we appreciate most about our girlfriends is their ability to make us laugh. Remember when she described a particularly god-awful blind date and you became so hysterical you spilled your iced coffee over *her* chicken salad? Or the time she made a funny non sequitur with a straight face during a tedious meeting with a client and you could barely suppress a very untimely giggle?

Even though we go to some friends for consolation, we are best served by those who restore our sense of humor and give us the courage to break free from our inhibitions.

Laughing with a friend is the best way to debunk our fear of being silly.

Between women friends, no small act of bravery ever goes unnoticed: no quirky comment is ever unappreciated, no spunky haircut is ever ignored, and no jaunty fashion statement is ever wasted. High-spirited women are unwitting role models, their actions a source of glee for other women who happen to know them.

See how great you feel the day you receive in the mail an

invitation to the gallery opening of a one-woman show featuring the paintings of your former boss.

Better yet, imagine leafing through a magazine at the beauty salon and stumbling across an article about a pioneering organic winemaker who single-handedly manages a prize-winning vineyard in California, only to discover that she is the woman with whom you shared a Lower East Side Manhattan walk-up right after college.

And be ready for the day when you turn on the TV and see on *Charlie Rose* a woman you befriended during a strenuous prebreakfast hike at a spa and who is now head of an international trade commission whose mandate is to rebuild Afghanistan.

Could I ever be like them? you wonder. Surprise, surprise. You already are as awesome as they are.

> Only a brave woman would have the courage to befriend a woman who is braver than she is.

If you think back, you'll realize that your childhood friends helped you become the person they themselves wanted to be: an audacious female with a heart of gold. At the same time, because you believed in them the way you did, they were able to display the dauntless spirit that made them special to you.

Remember: in nursery school, your best friend was a brat who wasn't afraid to punch boys who picked on her; in grade school, she was a loner who wrote sci-fi stories; in high school,

Laughing at ourselves is a form of bravery
we learn from friends.

she was a math major who painted her nails during chemistry class; in college, she was a self-proclaimed nonviolence activist who had changed her name from Emily to Bhikaji.

While you were admiring your friends' pluck, occasionally wishing that you too had the nerve to raise eyebrows as they did, you were becoming a gutsy lady, someone who respects the right of everyone to be bold and different.

And indeed, today, with your girlfriends, you don't feel compelled to be your sweet, cheerful, warm, and gregarious self. You can be the tough person who knows where she stands.

> You don't need the Miss Congeniality title: friendship is neither a popularity contest nor a beauty pageant.

You do not bank on your classic good looks or your sunny disposition to buy you much of anything in the world of female comradeship. You know that striving to be liked is probably the surest way to annoy the people you admire.

How liberating! With a girlfriend, prevailing standards of attractiveness are not a measure of your worth.

We can go about the business of befriending each other, knowing that if we were to tally all our pluses and minuses, no one would be better off.

One friend may have the sexiest hourglass figure, but she does not have your amazing sense of style. Another is a great hostess, but you are a much better fund-raiser and party organizer.

Overall, the good and the bad cancel each other out, and we all end up pretty much the same.

Liberty, equality, fraternity: the French got it right. Their formula for democracy stresses the fact that friendship between equals is the basis of a free society.

The pursuit of happiness is not an individual but a communal affair.

Epidemiology experts, who study health and disease patterns, have come to the conclusion that solidarity among citizens, more than material comfort, is the determining factor when it comes to everyone's well-being.

Apparently, less sexist societies tend to be healthier. As stated earlier, when women are happier and play a greater role in their community, their health, and the health of men and children, is better overall. And even though there is no

*Meet your sister at the airport
with a bouquet of flowers.*

consensus yet whether women's greater involvement is the cause or the effect of this improvement, why take a chance? While we wait for universal health coverage to become a reality, let's get together in a show of solidarity! Let's think of female camaraderie as a health insurance alternative.

Don't cancel that lunch date you made a month ago with a former colleague who never came back to work from maternity leave after she had her second child. Drag your hubby to the funky downtown club where the wife of a friend is performing for one night only as a stand-up comic. And meet your sister at the airport with a bouquet of flowers next time she flies over to visit you for the holidays.

• •

men
(VIVE LA DIFFÉRENCE!)

E V E N though we don't expect men to give up their seats or hold the door for us, we can't help but feel titillated when they do. Some ancient emotion is stirred when gender differences are tacitly celebrated.

The famous French expression *vive la différence!* (hooray for the difference!) takes the sting out of the disparity between men and women by highlighting the contrasts rather than the inequalities between the sexes.

"Why can't a woman be more like a man?" asks Professor Higgins in "A Hymn to Him," one of *My Fair Lady*'s most insightful lyrics. Why can't a woman be more like you, dear Henry? I can think of only two reasons.

First, if men and women were alike, there would be nothing to sing about, and no musical comedies with catchy tunes so memorable they become beloved cultural icons.

But even more detrimental to civilization would be the fact that women would have no incentive to call each other on the phone to talk about the fact that men don't call.

The war of the sexes is one of the most gallant wars there is, and probably the only one in which women have the advantage. If men and women were alike, there would be no one around to tell Higgins "I told you so." (At the end of *My Fair Lady*, Eliza doesn't need to tell him—he knows!)

Let's face it, the main difference between men and women is that women are usually right while men are usually wrong.

In all fairness, though, being right all the time becomes tedious after a while. But what's a girl to do? Men are so consistently disappointing, you suspect them of doing it on purpose. In fact, you sometimes wonder if their knack for making our hearts sink is a secondary male sex characteristic, like beards, chest hair, and deep voices.

Of late, the sensitive man is back on the endangered list. Guys play dumb as if to gall us. Nowadays, rare is the fellow who still acts as your best friend when he runs into his buddies, who knows what to say when your cat dies, who remembers to butter your toast when he brings you breakfast in bed, and who stays out of sight when he is wearing nothing but black socks and white boxer shorts.

By now, crushed romantic expectations are so much a part of the female experience that they have become a bonding force between women. The first *chagrin d'amour* is a rite of passage, the obligatory ordeal for a girl on the brink of adulthood. Only after she has survived that first sentimental disappointment is she part of the tribe. Her pout is less petulant, her brow less likely to express annoyance, and her gaze a shade darker behind her lashes. Other women can tell that she is no longer a child and tacitly welcome her into the fold.

So memorable is that first initiatory jilt that afterward she braces herself, always expecting the other shoe to drop. She lives in fear of being let down by men. She expects her dates, lovers, or husbands to screw up, and when the dear fellows prove inadequate, she is strangely gratified.

But what if the frustration between men and women were not a simple malfunction? What if it had a purpose? What if men's irritating behavior was motivated by a sincere desire to be helpful?

Before we declare men a nuisance, as they are sometimes characterized in the popular press, maybe we should stop and think. Granted, as a group they are antagonistic, but as individuals each one of them is a sweetheart.

The pesky sensation that a man is failing you *as if by design* deserves close examination.

One June day, when every flower stand is studded with opulent bouquets of peonies—your all-time favorite, their heavy blossoms as puffy as the cheeks of porcelain dolls—he brings home a meager bunch of daisies to make up for the fact that he is three hours late for dinner. You demand an explanation, but your man is not forthcoming, at least not for the time being. You rest your case by throwing the pathetic posies into a plastic tumbler and slamming the bedroom door in his face.

Only later will you find out the truth: he had learned that afternoon that his company was downsizing. He came home as late as he could to postpone sharing the bad news with you.

There is usually a perfectly good explanation for the way a man disappoints you, even though you might never find out what it is.

Let's say he joins an expensive health club but stops going there after the first few weeks. He stonewalls you when you needle him about it. Annoying? You bet. Yet you are better off

One thing men hate to hear is "We need to talk."

not knowing that he was developing a serious crush on his yoga instructor and decided to cool it before it was too late.

Men are under the impression that their job in life is to rescue women from impending danger. Is this why, when at long last he takes you to Paris, your man spends his afternoons watching the Tour de France on television in your hotel room? Take a wild guess. My bet is that he shuns museums because he doesn't want you to find out that you are traveling with someone who can't tell a Courbet from a Corot.

The peril a man is trying to save you from is himself. He is bent on rescuing you from the klutz he turns out to be when the sink springs a leak, the nervous wreck he becomes when you drive, the chauvinist who takes over the minute he gets hold of the TV remote, and the cheapskate who steps into a jewelry store around the time of your birthday.

He knows that you are going to blame him for not fixing things or not being there for you when you need him, but he would rather endure your wrath than hurt your feelings with some embarrassing revelation about one of his failings.

It's a paradox: a man will deliberately disappoint you in order not to disappoint you. But beware! The fact that his behavior makes no sense to you doesn't mean that you are right. It only means that there is a difference between you and him.

Old-fashioned gallantry may be dead, but most men are still chivalrous in their own way.

Even when he dumps his wife for someone half her age and exchanges the family car for a red convertible, a man will not look back in anger and hold his ex responsible for crushing his hopes.

Men disappoint women, but women don't disappoint men in quite the same way. It's not because women are better people, but because disappointment is not an emotion men know or understand. They experience rage, regret, remorse, but they seldom accuse the object of their former affection of being the cause of their downfall. For that reason alone men should be commended and given a special place in your heart.

So do not wait passively for a man to disappoint you. Counter his insecurities and self-deprecating impulses by reminding him why he is such a lovable human being.

Don't be caught off guard the next time he looks like he is about to let you down. Keep handy a mental list of all his qualities and pick appropriate—and inappropriate— moments to boost his fragile ego. Tell him you love the way he looks in a tux, for instance. Or extol the smell of his after-shave, his devotion to the kids, the allure of his new car, the fun you had last night raiding the icebox with him, and the fact that he can pry open tight jars and raw oysters.

> Assume that a man who disappoints you is
> a man asking for your attention.

Only when you deprive a man of his heroic role does he become frustrated with you—sometimes dangerously so.

A smart woman never impugns her significant other for wanting to be a knight in his imagination. If he promises to do something but does not deliver, she refrains from making a federal case of it. Only around the time of her birthday does she lay down some pretty explicit hints to thwart a major gaffe on his part and prevent a sentimental fiasco.

With each new disappointment, a woman grows stronger. Little by little, she frees herself from the idea that she needs her man to save her. If he fails to book the plane tickets, notify the utilities, or take out the trash, so be it. She reminds

As a group, men are predictable. But as individuals,
each one is a sweetheart.

herself that the father of her future children is a great dancer, a decent son-in-law, and an inspired weekend chef whose skills in the kitchen are evidence of his deep commitment to family life.

Eventually, a woman can learn not to be the one who is always right. Some loving wives have been known to lose an argument on purpose rather than say "I told you so." Others shamelessly start a conversation with their hubbies by cheerfully announcing, "You were absolutely right the other day. . . ." And Frenchwomen act coy at the dinner table: when their wineglass is empty, they don't help themselves but sweetly ask their man to refill it.

> Men set us free, one disappointment at a time.

The function of the knight-on-his-white-horse allegory is to help us deal with both fantasy and reality. Myths such as this one are instrumental in shaping our collective dreams, but their ulterior motive is to give us the means to wake up to the world as it is.

Only in fables are men the champions we make them out to be. In the end, though, all heroes must lose their status in order for them—and for us—to become fully realized human beings.

The next time a man falls short of your expectations, indulge in a little visualizing. Close your eyes and listen for the sound of a white horse galloping away. Imagine, clinging to its saddle, a lone rider clad in shining armor, visor down and banner in the wind. Admire the handsome spectacle before allowing this equestrian hallucination to disappear in a cloud of dust.

Have no regrets. A knight who disappoints a damsel does her the greatest favor—that of reminding her that she doesn't need to be rescued after all.

• •

sex
(EXCERPTS FROM CUPID'S
BAG OF TRICKS)

THE best-kept bedroom secret is this: a penis can read your
mind. With its X-ray vision, it can see through your thoughts
as clearly as it can see through your clothes.

It can tell when you are genuinely interested in a conversation, when you'd like to be asked to dance, when you think

it would be nice to be kissed, or when you wish the evening would never end.

When a penis figures out that you are in a receptive mood, it wants to prance, frolic, and romp. Its reaction is genuine joie de vivre, its surge is the expression of sheer exhilaration.

But that same penis is going to sulk when it finds out that you feel fat and ugly, that you are upset about your new haircut, or that you are worried about what you are going to wear at your sister's wedding.

A divining rod, a penis is easily spooked by what it perceives to be adverse psychological conditions. Potential partners who are overly self-conscious about their physical appearance make it nervous. A troll of sorts—the frog yet to become a prince—it is shy in the presence of those who put a premium on good looks.

Self-acceptance is sexy. To make a man swoon, change your thought pattern from anxious to generous.

So, in front of a man who desires you, hold off any self-denigrating thoughts about your physique—or about his anatomy. This is not the right time to explore your insecurities regarding your curves or list in your mind everything that is wrong with your breasts or your buttocks. Get a grip. Stand tall and trust that a man who is smitten with you is going to find you beautiful in the buff.

In survey after survey, women say that they want to look good for themselves, not to conform to men's expectations. The male journalists who report this information always express doubt: aren't women trying to seduce men anymore? Their comments show how little these men know about their own libido. Men are not attracted to women who are beautiful but to women who *feel* beautiful.

Irresistible is the woman who has reached a plateau in her quest for physical perfection and who is confident enough about her image to stop obsessing about it. She gives men the impression of being available for more challenging pursuits. No longer preoccupied with her appearance, she becomes accessible, attainable, vulnerable, desirable—in other words, sexy.

When it comes to lovemaking, men are in charge—they do the heavy lifting—but women take the initiative. The sleepy yawn of arousal in a banker's pinstriped trousers and the steely presence in the left leg of a young man's jeans are upbeat responses to neurological signals coming from a woman's brain. With just a thought (and a glance in his direction), she can, like Mae West, put a banana in the pocket of an unsuspecting fellow.

> In the arms of a woman, a man is always Cupid's apprentice.

Even a card-carrying macho man feels like a schoolboy when you take off your clothes. Men are clueless and they know it.

*Men must put up with the obsessive nature of the
maniac ensconced below their waist.*

They listen to each other boast about their sexual prowess, well aware that these tall tales are erotic fantasies even the most jaded Frenchman would find hard to believe.

With the exception of serious swingers, how many men have seen other men make love? Their main source of information comes from watching digital blondes with silicon implants fake orgasms with consenting adults whose fustian ardor can be truly alarming. No Shakespearean actors, the studs who perform in what used to be called Swedish art films can never translate the joy, the terror, and the torment of a lustful encounter, an event made even more confounding by the fact that we are grateful for the unspeakable hunger and thirst we experience in its jubilant throes.

Additionally, canned erotica never tells men what they *really* want to know, namely, how women feel when they first see their lover's erect penis. Do they share his awe at the sudden materialization of his most grandiose urges? Size is not the only issue: what about the color, the angle, and the savor of the lurching giant?

And, pray tell, how do you manage when all you have to show for it is what the great Latin poet Catullus, with his raw sense of humor, described as "a tiny dagger, drooping like a flabby parsnip"?

Pity the men. Whether they like it or not, they must put up with the idiosyncrasies of the maniac ensconced below their waist. Nature gives them no choice but to accommodate the selfish-gene obsession of this permanent guest.

Great sex is not a tête-à-tête but a threesome between a man, his penis, and the loving partner who inspires the two of them to show some esprit de corps.

From kings' mistresses to late-night-TV sex therapists, initiating men to the subtle art of love is a role women have ardently embraced throughout history. Unlike professionals, though, it is not advisable for you and I to try to initiate our lovers by flaunting our expertise. A little coquetry is necessary. An ordinary woman who is too knowledgeable might ruffle a man's sensibility.

It's best to teach by example. Though she can guide his hand in the heat of passion, a female sex partner is never as graphic as when she illustrates a point with a little story she has gleaned from talking with other women.

"In knowledge of such things we are babes compared to women," wrote the Renaissance French philosopher Michel de Montaigne in one of his most famous essays. "Listen to women describe our rendezvous with them, and you will quickly realize that we contribute nothing to the topic they didn't already know."

Like Montaigne, most men today would be quite surprised if they could be the proverbial fly on the wall. "I happened to be one day in a place where my ear could unsuspectedly catch part of what they were saying to each other," added the bewildered essayist. "I wish I could tell you!"

The things we tell each other are not meant to stay *entre nous*. Share them with the man in your life to enlighten him about the intricacies of your libido.

In order to pique the curiosity of the sultan Shahriyar—and open his heart in the process—Scheherazade, the heroine of *Arabian Nights,* pretended to allow him to eavesdrop on the stories she told her sister. You can use the same stratagem with your significant other. Give him the impression that he is on the inside track by feeding him risqué tidbits stolen from one of your girlfriends' amusing off-the-record tales.

Weave together straight narration and personal asides as you recount a conversation you had that afternoon with a very good friend about the way her husband likes to take her impromptu on top of his desk at home. Evoke, with a sweeping gesture and a glint in your eye, how he pushes aside books and papers to make room for their disorderly passion!

Before your lover has time to form an opinion of your friend's indiscretion, up the ante with a story within a story, another technique Scheherazade favored to counteract her listener's masculine tendency to look for closure—to prematurely come to a climax, so to speak. Postponing the conclusion of a tale (and keeping a man guessing) is a great metaphor for delaying the premature denouement of lovemaking.

So confide to him that you could not stop laughing when

that same friend told you in great detail how, the previous weekend, she caught her sister and her new boyfriend in flagrante delicto in their parents' pantry. Tell him how the two of them were entwined in such a way as to form a six-legged creature with two arms and two heads—one of which was upside down.

A man needs to know that for a woman there is a lot more to sex than his own performance.

The spirit, the mood, the humor, the setting, and the particular circumstances are just as important to you as the physical attributes of the anatomical part of his body that sometimes behaves as his second brain.

A penis is a stubborn and narcissistic creature, and the art of love consists in setting a man free from the demands of this little tyrant. Rather than worry about the libido of your sex partner, try to release him from performance anxiety by showing little concern for your own carnal exploits.

There is no "doing" in great sex. Even the most acrobatic positions feel effortless, their glorious configuration as unpredictable as the accidental patterns created by the prisms of a kaleidoscope.

Never trust appearances alone. Love is blind—so is lovemaking: show a man what he can only see with his eyes closed.

What is happening between two people in bed is usually best described by metaphors. Before the invention of mirrors—and video cameras—sexual intercourse was a blind foray into a sightless world.

Indeed, as suitors get physically closer to each other, they progressively lose eye contact. With the woman's body now inches away from his face, a man naturally shifts his attention from the magnificent spectacle of his manhood to the variegated realm of his other senses.

> Turning off the light helps us turn on our
> extrasensory perceptions.

Paradoxically, the obscurity brings about a new kind of vision. Groping hands are great visualizing devices. In the dark, the beauty of the other person ceases to be just an optical phenomenon.

Unable to see who they embrace, with no depth of field, no sense of height or width, the grateful lovers are released from the cubical prison of the third dimension.

Free of such notions as "yours" and "mine," inside and outside, convex and concave, they keel over in one blurred motion, capsizing bottom side up, clutching, kissing, grabbing, sputtering, squirming, shivering—the space between their bodies an amorous magnetic field strong enough to generate in their minds the equivalent of a spectacular aurora light show.

self-improvement
(THE SEVEN DEADLY VIRTUES)

*Beware of purity and incorruptibility . . . and all the
other seven deadly virtues.*

OSCAR WILDE

IMAGINE putting your feet up on your desk, leaning back,
crossing your hands behind your neck, and deciding once and
for all to stop agonizing over the fact that the world is going
to hell in a handbasket.

Don't get me wrong: I am not suggesting that you wear rose-colored glasses, just that you refrain from taking everything personally. You would not want to make a virtue out of being incensed or outraged.

Don't blame anyone—yourself included—for not doing enough to stamp out injustice, expose corruption, eradicate fraud, or eliminate waste. Try to steer clear of the deadly sense of respectability that comes from occupying the moral high ground.

Righteous indignation, though justifiable, makes as many victims as the crimes it castigates. It robs you of your sense of humor and leaves you feeling powerless and crabby.

But what about fighting for progress? you may ask. Shouldn't you try to uphold high standards and make things better overall? Cast aside this idea for a while. The ancient Greeks and Romans, who have never been labeled underachievers, did not make progress an issue. Yet they invented Western civilization as we know it—their accomplishments in politics, the arts, philosophy, and mathematics continue to inform today's culture. Even so, there is not a single reference to progress in any of their books.

Of course, you still applaud six-lane highways, online shopping, wireless laptops, wonder drugs, high-definition TV, instant messaging, electronic ticketing, and microsurgery— but you no longer believe that these inventions are technological breakthroughs that will save our species from extinction. If you didn't take for granted that progress is an amelioration, you could choose to let well enough alone and forgo self-improvement—your weird idiosyncrasies forever part and parcel of the nature of all carbon-based life-forms, of which you are a perfect example.

> An upgrade is progress, though not always an improvement.

What would happen if you felt under no pressure whatsoever to correct your behavior or improve your disposition? Would the world come to an end if you stubbornly kept the same hairdo for years, held on to your frayed underpants, never got over your fear of small dogs, managed to avoid telling your shrink the truth about your sex life, systematically dated the wrong kind of men, sent chain letters to unsuspecting friends, and felt no shame when taking a second helping of mashed potatoes?

Our character flaws become qualities when we endure them graciously. In contrast, laborious excellence can easily turn sour. We quickly resent those among us who work hard at being good. "Some people are likable in spite of their unswerving integrity," quipped the legendary New York columnist Don Marquis. Let's face it, though, they are the exception.

To stay on the safe side—and challenge the assumption that progress is our only salvation—a comprehensive list of deadly virtues might be a valuable tool.

ASSUMING THAT ONE IS NEVER TOO THIN OR TOO RICH

If we didn't feel obliged to become a better person—thinner, smarter, healthier—we would have no use for inflated superlatives. No "Most Livable Cities in the United States" or "World's Greatest Chefs." No "Worst Crimes of the Century" or "Most Celebrated Gossip Columnist."

Furthermore, we would buy more steamy novels than quick-fix self-help books, so there would be practically no risk of anyone's trying to become skinny, punctual, patient, compassionate, or wealthy overnight.

Because ratings would have no currency, sophisticated world travelers would never show off by professing publicly to prefer London to Paris, Los Angeles to San Francisco, or Brussels to Venice. And, needless to say, best-dressed socialites would be way too thin and much too rich.

Real progress, in our culture, would be figuring out when enough is enough.

When to curb our greed—and be willing to pay higher taxes if it would improve public education.

When to restrain our ambition—and not volunteer to join the co-op's lobby-redecorating committee or host the hiking club's welcome-new-members party.

When to put our family first—and say to the boss, "Sorry, Frank. I gotta go."

To paraphrase Ogden Nash, the problem with progress is that it has gone on too long.

CONSTANTLY RAISING THE BAR

People should be encouraged to set goals for themselves, strive to reach them, and when they make good, have a little party. The preferred way to celebrate a raise, for instance, would be to open a good bottle of champagne, get together with the guys in the mail room, invite the cute administrative assistant, and make an ass of oneself by telling bad jokes.

Fat chance. The corporate world is designed to keep you on the up-and-up. Along with the bonuses and the promotions come the gold watch (these days, it is encrusted with diamonds), the invitation to play golf at Coronado in San Diego, and the one-on-one sessions with an image consultant.

Before you know it, the perks are taking over your life. You are in big trouble when, for the holidays, you are flown with ninety-nine of your company's top performers and their spouses to Prague. After a performance of *The Nutcracker* on the Charles Bridge (transformed into a stage for the occasion), you are invited to attend a candlelight state dinner at the Prague Castle hosted by the minister of culture of the Czech Republic, who is a friend of your CEO's.

All the fuss and travel makes you nostalgic for the staid office Christmas parties of yesteryear, during which you sang carols with the IT platform manager and the HR benefits vendor around the rented Steinway. In a snapshot of you taken at one of those obligatory events by a bleary-eyed colleague, you look unexpectedly pretty, relaxed and happy in the silly blue velvet dress with puffy sleeves you bought at Macy's.

In hindsight, progressing up the ladder is easy. What is difficult is to still be happy by the time you get to the top.

Third Deadly Virtue

HAVING WHAT IT TAKES

Let's not confuse "living well" with "getting ahead." There is more to survival than simply competition. An ability to adapt and take advantage of unexpected mutations is just as critical. In fundamental research—as opposed to clinical tests—what is least expected is most likely to occur. Anticipating good results is bad science. The best way to serve your selfish genes is not to overcome all obstacles, but rather be on the lookout for surprises.

Don't be so focused on your performance that you ignore the world around you. Step back from time to time in order to see the big picture and perhaps come across brand-new perceptions. If you are a type A personality, pretend to be a type B: Deliberately stop to smell the electricity in the air before a storm, for instance. Lie down on the carpet for no reason and stare at the ceiling. Make eye contact with a baby. Get up from your chair to turn off the air conditioner and open a window. Interrupt your train of thought to watch the twitching whiskers of a sleeping cat.

One can affirm life without affirming one's determination and will to succeed.

Fourth Deadly Virtue

WASTING NO TIME

Unproductive time is a luxury few of us feel we can afford. We are personally annoyed—even offended—by our own inefficiency as if it were a sign of some basic incompetence. Yet mechanical filibustering is widespread, and even the most sophisticated time-saving devices are incapable of eradicating the phenomenon. Appliances break down. Computers crash. Cell phones go dead. No matter how good our technology, blunders are here to stay.

A sure way to become chronically frustrated is to put excessive value on every god-sent instant.

Instead of waiting passively for the next screwup to disrupt your tight schedule, be proactive and preemptively mis-

Interrupt your train of thought to watch the twitching whiskers of a sleeping cat.

spend precious minutes. Every so often, give the prodigal universe five seconds of your time: throw away the stray plastic paper clips that got mixed up with the metal ones; dust the hinges of your laptop; refold the dish towels in the linen closet; or, when no one is looking, tap your fingernails rhythmically on the table or roll your eyes dramatically, in mock exasperation.

In other words, disable little annoyances before they disable you.

BEING ORGANIZED

Of the many little flaws that plague our lives, being disorganized is probably one of the most pleasurable.

There is something strangely liberating about forgetting a name, a word, or a date. In a mental landscape momentarily deprived of familiar markers, the world feels suddenly less crowded.

It often happens when you should be rushing out of the house to get to an appointment on time. You find yourself ransacking the place looking for God knows what. You rummage through the pockets of your raincoat, the kitchen drawer, and the medicine cabinet in search of . . . your grocery list? your cough drops? your umbrella? the reason you're going out in the first place?

Caught in a temporal cul-de-sac, unable to move forward or back, one can get a glimpse of "the other side," the parallel universe of geological time.

Stay there for a moment and imagine that you can feel the imperceptible movement of tectonic plates and the majestic rotation of planets overhead.

Come to think of it, disorganization is not a bad way to slow down the otherwise relentless ticking of the clock.

BEING GOAL-ORIENTED

Knowing what you want, and getting it, can deprive you of the pleasure of having a deliciously unproductive afternoon. Consider an intriguing alternative: knowing what you want, and then finding out that you don't want it after all.

It goes this way: You leave the house on Saturday with the idea of buying the latest espresso maker, a set of ergonomic pillows, and a new lighting fixture for the living room. After an hour perusing the housewares department, you burn out and decide you've got way too many choices and way too much stuff already. Going home empty-handed, you feel uncharacteristically elated. You stroll down the avenue with your hands squarely in your pockets, whistling the first four notes of Elvis's "Love Me Tender."

Keep in mind that fruitless errands can be the source of great spiritual satisfaction. You would have to meditate for months in a Zen monastery to come to the sudden realization that you are happy with what you already have. Understandably, for penniless monks, achieving a blissful state of "not-wanting" is more of a challenge than for you and I, who have only to walk through a megamall to come to the same conclusion.

*Don't deprive yourself of the pleasure of having
an unproductive afternoon.*

Losing one's desire to have it all can be a blessing in disguise. The trancelike state of materialistic overload we experience in such occasions is what Buddhists call satori.

BEING RIGHTEOUS

As mentioned earlier, feeling smug is antithetical to joie de vivre. So if there is something not quite wonderful about you, get over it. Accept that you are a human being—somebody neither all good nor all bad.

That said, don't go overboard in the opposite direction: all things considered, it is better to be a perfectionist riddled with self-criticisms than someone who flaunts her imperfections as if they were personal trophies.

In this arrogant category are individuals who boast about not liking children, who pad their résumés, who blame others for their shortcomings, who dress casually for funerals, who have never said "I'm sorry" to someone weaker than they are, who call your current boyfriend "What's-his-name," who say they could never work for a woman, and who do not own an unabridged dictionary.

Yes, it is better to believe in progress, as flawed a proposition as it is, than to be the kind of person who presumes that her character flaws are above the fray.

Foolish optimism is not a deadly virtue.

• •

homemaking
(HOW TO HAVE SOME GOOD CLEAN FUN)

"**MAKE** yourself at home," says the hostess to her weekend guests. She directs them to their room, where there is a freshly made bed, a pile of neatly folded towels on a chair, fluffed-up pillows on the settee, and a bud vase with three garden roses on the nightstand. Not a speck of dust dances in the rays of sunlight coming through the windows, and the pale yellow rug is as groomed as the coat of a French poodle.

One of the reasons we love going to other people's houses is to get away from the mess at home! The degree of neatness we find there is often a measure of how welcomed we feel. It is a treat to visit friends whose household gives an impression of serene tidiness—there, we can fool our senses into believing that everyday life is an orderly affair.

But can keeping a house blissfully neat ever be the effortless act the perfect hostess makes it seem to be, or is it only in fairy tales that women clean and scrub for the joy of it, for the fleeting pleasure of putting everything in its place?

In real life, the psychological rewards of domestic upkeep usually come after the fact. We believe that the best part of it all is the result—the release of endorphins brought about by the sight of a recently vacuumed rug or that of a scrubbed bathroom. Only when the floors are shiny, the dishes are put away, the beds are made, and the bathroom sink is sparkling do we reap the benefits of not being a slob.

Seldom do we think of the endeavor itself as a joyful event. We hold our breath, figuratively and sometimes even literally, until we've completed all the menial tasks housecleaning entails. Are we missing out on something? Like taking care of a pet, loving a child, or raising a family, can making a home be an end in itself rather than a means? In other words, can buffing and polishing the things we love and have worked so hard to assemble be the source of genuine contentment?

Think again: sometimes all it takes is a dust
cloth to turn rags into riches.

Labor-saving devices have simplified life to the point where very few activities nowadays require your total, unconditional physical involvement.

Some things, though, will never be completely sweat-free. Two of them in particular: lovemaking and housecleaning! Try as you might to avoid exertion, they both require the full participation of your body as well as your mind.

Sex and dust have one thing in common: they resist automation. They don't come with a cruise-control option.

Sure, some of the latest robotic vacuum cleaners have been engineered to run on their own, and vibrators promise to deliver technologically assisted climaxes. But no remote can scour the top of the stove for you, nor can it make the earth move under your feet.

Mercifully, digitalization and nanotechnologies have not completely eradicated the analog world of sheer materiality. A home is still the very real envelope in which we curl up at night in search of security and physical comfort. Instinctively, as we move around the house, we pat, stroke, and touch the objects in it the same way we pat, stroke, and touch the people with whom we live.

This kinetic rapport is an act of appropriation. When you care for a house with your own hands, you claim ownership of the place. Tidying up the linen closet, dusting the spice rack, or even just wiping clean a countertop is like putting your name on the door.

Your home is an intimate partner: treat it as you would a lover.

Sexually suggestive expressions like "having some good clean fun" or "getting down and dirty" are further evidence of the blurring of the line between two exercises that get us into compromising positions.

Indeed, the contortions necessary to chase dust bunnies are on a par with some risqué *Kama Sutra* practices. And while no one objects to getting on one's hands and knees in the name of cleanliness, some of us might hesitate to do the same thing in the name of Eros.

In the past, cleaning was invested with an erotic subtext (the fantasy of the French maid a living vestige), but cleaning today has been cleansed of all sexual innuendos, with housekeeping now presented to the American housewife as pure drudgery.

But would we be as resentful of having to do the laundry, put away the dishes, and mop the floor if we had not been told over and over that it's a drag to waste time scrubbing away when we could actually be having fun?

Victims of what amounts to a repressive campaign, most of us take for granted that cleaning house is a dirty business. We have been intimidated into wearing tattered clothing

Cleaning house is good clean fun,
even if you have a dirty mind.

when picking up a broom, as if dressing like a busboy was part of the job. Looking like hell, we labor under the impression that we are Cinderella stuck at home while our pampered stepsisters are going to the ball.

Change your attitude toward housecleaning by changing out of your ragged work clothes.

Don't subscribe to the idea that you are going to get dirty by cleaning your house. Most cleansers nowadays look and smell like they belong in a spa. Aromatherapy helping, household products are gentler than ever. The cavernous space under the kitchen sink where you keep cleaning fluids is no longer filled with poisonous brews. Mops and brooms have also gone through a technological makeover—they are now slender, weightless, and a snap to use. No self-respecting old witch would want to be caught riding across the night sky on one of these effete, newfangled sweepers.

So take off your stained T-shirt. Peel off those ugly latex gloves. Shun your scuffed sneakers. Slip instead into a nice dress and put on a pair of heels. Tie your hair back with a scarf or a ribbon. Put on a pretty apron. Pick up a feather duster and waltz across the room as if guided by some invisible hand.

You are going to have a ball.

Figuring out how to clean a house efficiently is not unlike mastering the complex steps of a quadrille, a fox-trot, or a tango.

Take dance lessons from Cinderella.

Cinderella must have been in fantastic shape. An accomplished housekeeper by all accounts, she was nimble on her feet, her ability to traipse around in glass slippers proof positive of her stamina and poise.

Apparently her sex appeal was as formidable as her muscular endurance. Sweeping dirt was no impediment to sweeping the most eligible bachelor in the fairy-tale kingdom off his feet.

Not a prude, but someone who did get down and dirty, our cinder-girl was the victim of prejudices against housework that are pretty much universal—and as old as humanity. Already, in eighth-century China, a popular folktale told the story of a handmaiden with tiny feet whose rags-to-riches saga is the original Cinderella story. Like her Western counterpart, the Chinese heroine rises from the ashes at the end of the story to affirm her purity.

According to the late celebrated psychiatrist Bruno Bettelheim, who gathered insight on child development from a careful analysis of fairy tales, Cinderella's pristine slipper, a symbol of virginity tucked in the pocket of her soiled apron, is yet another allusion to the apparent contradiction between clean and dirty.

Likewise, tucked inside the convoluted plot of this most-beloved fairy tale is a coded message: the dirt we handle when we clean house does not sully us, just as great sex does not defile our body.

Being physical is sexy. Cleaning house can be
a seamless choreography of harmonious gestures.

Eye-hand coordination is essential when one is scurrying
around, but so is right-side/left-side coordination. One of
the pleasures of cleaning is to restore balance and harmony,

Think of cleaning as beautifying your home.

externally as well as internally. Encourage the right side and the left side of your body to work as a team, and your right-brain/left-brain circuitry begins to hum blissfully.

Before you begin, give one hand the task of helping the other and watch them collaborate under your supervision. Hands love to work in unison. One hand will steady the cutting board while the other cleans it; one hand will pat down the laundry while the other folds it. They even seem to think on their own, without having to be prompted. As soon as one hand is done with a job, for instance, the other is ready to start the next. With the last cup in the dishwasher, the left hand volunteers to close the door to give the right hand time to position itself on the start knob.

Manual competence can do a lot for your self-esteem— light housekeeping sometimes can act as a form of mental therapy. When you are stressed or preoccupied, try emptying wastebaskets or polishing the dining room table. Even the smallest deed, like putting a book back on a shelf or changing a lightbulb, can set your mind at ease.

> Often, the difference between grunt work and domestic bliss is a matter of perspective.

Think of cleaning as beautifying a room. Grabbing a dust cloth, a sponge, or a brush is usually motivated by a desire to make things look good. Cleaning is an impulse to paint a pretty picture.

Call upon your artistic sense: As you scrub and mop, squint like a painter in front of a canvas. Take advantage of the available light to make sure that you are doing a swell job. Hold glasses up to the light when drying them. Open up the blinds before waxing the floor. Sit by the window to polish the silver.

For painters as well as homemakers, light is the primary source of inspiration. Spring cleaning is prompted by the fact that the days are longer and the inside of the house is brighter.

One could make a case that the main objective of housekeeping is not to sanitize the place but to ensure that sunlight is not sullied by dirt or dust when it lands on the floor and the furniture.

With the angle of illumination changing as Earth rotates around the Sun, shedding light upon a nook here and a cranny there depending on the season, rare are the corners of your house that do not get a once-a-year look over.

On a particular spring day, for instance, the light will be just right and you will see previously invisible smudges on the side of the icebox.

One summer evening, in the glow of sunset, you will notice cobwebs above the bookcase.

One morning in late September, a ray of sun will bounce off your neighbor's window in such a way as to illuminate the dust accumulated under your piano.

Home is a safe haven on the edge of chaos.

These cursory sightings are invitations to take immediate action. Deal with unexpected eyesores at once. Interrupt whatever you happen to be doing to direct the nozzle of a squirt bottle at a mildew stain, give the back of a faucet a good scrub with an old toothbrush, or grab a tissue to dust the top of a picture frame.

Clean on impulse and you'll always be one step ahead of the mess. Being systematically spontaneous is efficient.

We often postpone taking care of small messes to avoid being perceived as compulsive. Who wants to be called a control freak? It's better to be compared to Oscar Madison than to Felix Unger! In our laid-back culture, a slob is more endearing than a neatnik.

Fool everyone into thinking that you are a nonchalant homemaker by never displaying your domestic skills in front of others. As the saying goes, "Don't wash your dirty laundry in public."

Housekeeping—like sex, indeed—is not supposed to be a group activity. It is most enjoyable when done in private. One would be as self-conscious vacuuming a rug in front of an audience as one would be passionately kissing one's hubby when people are watching. So, whenever company's around, put away the laundry basket, hide your squirt bottles under the sink, and don't go around straightening pictures on the wall.

A graceful hostess does not apologize for the mess. She leaves well enough alone to concentrate on welcoming her guests.

In fact, the expression "make yourself at home" is an open invitation for guests to make a mess of their own. The minute they walk in, they are given the implicit permission to take off their coats, unwind, unpack if need be, and put their feet up. Within minutes of their arrival, you can expect your living room to be in shambles and their bedroom to look like a camping ground.

So be it. Your home is not a pristine showroom for your ego but a safe haven on the edge of chaos. It is a place where one can crawl between rumpled sheets with a cup of tea and a plate piled high with warm buttery toast. Even in the best-kept houses, there is a time and a place for bread crumbs in the shag rug and smeared jam on the pillowcases.

Shrug your shoulders as I do when disorder prevails over your desperate attempts to contain it. Heck, if things never got messy, one would never experience the pleasure of making them neat again, and the sweet satisfaction of getting everything back under control.

• •

pretty things
(IN PRAISE OF FRIVOLITY)

FROM individually wrapped chocolates in gold-foil boxes to alluring fragrances in sealed eau de toilette bottles and diamond rings nestled in tightly shut jewel cases, pretty things are often kept in secured containers as if to protect potential users against some hazardous substance.

Innocuous at first glance, pretty things are in fact powerful antidepressants. You can get addicted to having them around. The wide availability of pretty things in France is the reason joie de vivre is so endemic to the culture. People are literally hooked on the stuff. All one needs to do is walk down the street and glance at the display of gemlike pastries in the window of a patisserie to instantly experience an elevated sense of contentment.

The universal appeal of French products is a well-established fact, the magnet that attracts tourists who want a taste of the good life. But wherever the puritan ethic prevails, the status of pretty things is equivocal. The word *pretty* has an Old English root meaning *tricky, artful, deceitful*. As a result, here, in America, one is rather suspicious of things that are deliberately pretty. Calling something pretty can be construed as a put-down. "Pretty nice" means only "so-so" and "pretty much over" doesn't leave much room for hope.

Over time, in what was presumably an attempt to downplay the irresistible charm of pretty things, the word used to designate them was tempered to mean "nice, but lacking strength, force, manliness, purpose, or intensity" (*Webster's*). Don't be fooled by this lame definition, though. The spontaneous oohs and aahs that pretty things elicit is evidence of the very strong hold these objects have on us.

And indeed, even urbane types like you and me who profess to be minimalists and are partial to form and function are not completely immune to the frivolity of the material world.

We can't help but experience a flutter in our chest at the sight of a lacquered découpage platter with a floral border, a cashmere throw pillow embellished with quail-feather trims, or a rose-quartz necklace with gold swags spangled with sapphire briolettes.

> Take the time to look at pretty things:
> savor those materialistic
> rewards that money can't buy.

Even if you are a modern girl who doesn't care much for doilies, gingerbread, or pom-poms, you may want to put your misgivings aside for a while and consider the following: pretty trappings can entrap you indeed, but it's for your own good.

Pretty things have the unique ability to make us feel not only upbeat but also receptive. We become surprisingly open-minded in their presence. It would take a hardened modernist not to be pleasantly affected by the sight of a delicate silk rose pinned to a large straw hat, engraved stationery printed on vellum as crisp as Stoned Wheat Thins, or little girls' party dresses adorned with exquisite velvet appliqués.

Even if you'd never buy any of that fancy stuff, you can't help but stare at it. It's not about acquisition but appreciation. Some pretty things are not meant to be bought but merely admired. Even though you may never dream of spending a small fortune to own a pair of Murano blue-glass chandeliers or hang chinoiserie wallpaper in your dining room, you are glad some folks are rich enough to afford such things so that they can be displayed in store windows, picture books, and interior design magazines.

Think of appreciation as a pleasant alternative to ownership.

Unlike other forms of appreciation (art, poetry, music, or wine), there is no learning curve with pretty things. They reach out to us, regardless of our education, experience, or taste. You don't have to be a connoisseur to admire the perfection of a silver saltshaker that looks like a miniature pagoda, to be seduced by the loveliness of a garden-fresh bridal bouquet, or to marvel at the slim beauty of a diamond-studded Art Deco bracelet watch.

In other words, you don't treat a pretty thing the same way you would treat a wine at a tasting. You are not trying to assess the subtle color and complex bouquet of a Merlot, a Syrah, or a Pinot Noir. It's much simpler than that: you can almost measure prettiness in inches and seconds. To deserve this appellation, an object must persuade you to (1) draw near and (2) linger. Its small details compel you to come closer, within eight to twelve inches of it, while its intricate patterns capture your attention for at least thirty seconds.

It is mainly a question of scale. As intimate objects, not to be confused with luxury products that broadcast their status

The more time you give to pretty things,
the more pleasure you get.

through a system of eye-catching signs that must be recognizable at a glance (you can spot that famous LV logo on an accessory from far away), pretty things do not often reveal their identity readily. They rely on delicate patterns and fine textures to alert you to their presence. You slow down and eventually stop to figure out what they are. Like interactive devices, they engage you on a one-to-one basis.

A bow is not unlike a heart: It turns a gift into an intimate offering.

It's a give-and-take arrangement: the more time you give to pretty things, the more pleasure you can take away. Rather than bring out our greed or acquisitiveness, they stimulate our curiosity and invite us to share our sense of wonder with others.

> Handle pretty things with care:
> they will stir your emotions.

If you succumb to the charm of a particularly enticing object and decide to purchase it, be prepared to give it away eventually. You won't be able to resist, and it will feel good. It is in the very nature of pretty things to circulate among people, and sooner or later you will be tricked into handing the treasure over to someone else as a gift.

One day, a good friend will admire the beaded chiffon scarf you got a week earlier in a little boutique in your neighborhood; impulsively, you will take it off your neck and give it to her.

Or a dinner guest will call you to thank you for last night's party and ask you, in the course of the conversation, where you bought those pretty enameled napkin rings. "Ten years ago, in Madrid," you'll tell her—and make up your mind on the spot to send them to her as a belated birthday present.

Most likely, though, you will decide who will be the lucky recipient of your self-indulgence even before you pay for it.

Unable to resist the enticement of a carved music box, for instance, you will earmark it as a future gift for your niece.

Not all your pretty belongings belong to you. Some of them are destined to be gift wrapped.

In traditional societies, some things were simply commodities while others were endowed with a "spirit" and destined to function as gifts. Invested with a symbolic meaning, these precious ritualistic objects would pass from hand to hand within a community, and with each donation the network of complex social relationships would be strengthened.

All gifts come with strings attached. They create an obligation to reciprocate. This is a paradox that has philosophers and social scientists arguing back and forth forever. Though gifts are not altruistic after all, scholars nonetheless agree that they foster between people an intimate dialogue, on a personal rather than a commercial basis.

When we lovingly tie a pretty ribbon around a box containing a gift, we affirm the importance of this personal connection. If, on top of it, we secure a large bow, we add a strong emotional component to the transaction.

A bow is not unlike a heart. It even looks like one. The two strands of the knot cross over, the same way the arteries and the veins cross over in the middle of the chest. This similarity between the shape of the heart and that of a bow could explain why gift wrapping is more than surface decoration.

With the bundle of pretty frills that surrounds a gift, you joyfully offer your throbbing heart, each curl of the ribbon coiled like the cavities through which your blood courses and your life ebbs and flows.

• •

makeovers
(PARISIAN BEAUTY SECRETS)

WE all know that beauty is in the eye of the beholder. In Paris, my hometown, this truism is taken literally to mean that no one is ever unattractive. And even though blond hair, blue eyes, and high cheekbones are not negligible attributes, they are by no means the measure of your beauty.

There, an alluring woman who is not conventionally pretty is revered as a *jolie laide*—literally an ugly belle—and she is often the object of envy because of her uncanny ability to attract suitors in spite of her unusual looks. In Paris, beauty is the blurry silhouette of two revelers sharing an umbrella as they run to catch the last *métro*. It is the expression of glee on the face of a baby who sees a puppy for the first time. It is what happens in the moist, pitch-dark theater of the brain when you think of a loved one.

In my hometown, beauty is not a physical quality but a joyful phenomenon at the intersection of mind and matter, thoughts and flesh, firing neurons and watery cells.

Likewise, beauty products are not just a means to an end. They are not mere prescriptions whose visible results can be measured. In reality, a visit to the cosmetics counter is a holistic event. It is an experience that stimulates one's sensory perceptions and with them the delicate nerve paths that link the surface of the body to the mysterious recesses of the soul.

Beauty is a feeling, not a spectacle.

If you have recently bought a lipstick, you've noticed that the girl behind the counter had to scurry around to find a mirror for you to test the product. One would assume that cosmetics departments would not be lacking in reflective surfaces. Not true. Handheld mirrors are kept in drawers while the few freestanding models on the counters are placed so low there is no way you can see your face in them unless you happen to be four feet tall.

Why is it virtually impossible for you to catch a casual look at yourself as you negotiate your way around the sparkling displays?

Realistically speaking, a startling encounter with your plain reflection would have a negative effect on your spending mood. If you could see yourself in the blinding artificial light that showcases the beauty products, chances are you would be tempted to turn around and run in the opposite direction.

But there is another reason, not quite as mundane: people in the beauty business are not about to let you gaze at your own image—not until you are in the right frame of mind. They know that, first and foremost, cosmetics make you *feel* beautiful. They improve your self-image before improving your looks.

With their sensuous textures, seductive scents, luscious colors, and suggestive shapes, makeup and skin-care products awaken our dormant artistic emotions. The wonderwork of cosmetics is to create that very special sense of elation associated with refinement, taste, and beauty. Open a jar of delicately fragrant lotion and your right hemisphere lights up. Almost instantaneously your aesthetic appreciation takes priority over your rational judgment.

In other words, the active ingredients in an ounce of

supermoisturizing lift cream are not some high-tech molecules but the neurotransmitters in your brain.

Love your body—and Frenchmen will love you.

In America, nine out of ten women are not happy with their physique. The great anatomical wonder that is their naked self is a burden to most of them. In France, where women are under less pressure to be thin, a rotund silhouette is seldom reason enough to renounce the pleasure of a daily baguette. And whereas losing ten pounds in the United States requires a full-fledged campaign, getting rid of the equivalent four and a half kilos seems less taxing in metric system parlance: smaller numbers give French dieters a definite psychological advantage over their American counterparts.

If you need a break from counting pounds and calories, consider a trip to Paris. Drop your bags at your hotel and make a beeline for the nearest public garden. A stroll through the Tuileries or the Luxembourg, where statues of curvy women in minimal attire frolic behind manicured bushes, might be just the thing to reconcile your eye with the look of classically proportioned figures.

But wait: whereas the conventional assumption is that nudity in art was the product of male lechery, some investigative minds are proposing a different interpretation. According to revisionist art critiques, the display of nude female

You are awesome when you embrace your statuesque figure.

bodies was a deliberate attempt to prop up women's self-esteem and rouse their libido as much as to titillate the fancy of their male companions.

Since the early days of the Renaissance, men understood that a woman who loves her body is a more playful bedmate than one who is overly self-conscious of her physical flaws. The scantily dressed marble figures in courtyards and alleys, on the facades of buildings, and in the middle of reflecting pools were all fleshy role models, their generous curves made more evident by the folds of loosely held garments.

Today, I cannot imagine American couples emulating their European ancestors and hanging paintings of prosperous-looking nudes on the walls of their bedrooms. Neither would they approve of sleeping under ceilings decorated with heavy plaster moldings featuring chubby ladies tussling with equally chubby cupids.

But for them there is Air France and sundry romantic weekend deals that include free passes to the Louvre, the Orsay museum, the Maillol foundation, and Versailles.

An alert mind is the most eye-catching feature of a face.

The weight of a blank expression pulls your face down like gravity. Quick, think of something pleasant—anything—and your physiognomy brightens. An intriguing idea crossing your mind can lift the muscles of your face more than an application of firming cream.

You can almost trace the energizing action of a thought from its point of departure near the roots of your hair, down to the sides of your forehead where the skin tightens, to the tiny muscles around your eyes that constrict as you focus on some internal vision. All this activity raises your cheeks slightly and teases the corners of your mouth—the prelude of a smile, perhaps—giving the contour of your jaw a sharper definition.

For the Parisian woman, putting herself together in the morning is first and foremost a mental act. She starts thinking the minute she looks in her mirror. She'll reexamine something someone said the day before, kick around a couple of alternatives for what to cook for dinner, or flirt with the idea of changing her hair color. Before she gets around to brushing her hair and putting on her makeup, she already has developed "an attitude," a strong opinion about how to best conduct her life.

Sure, she'll get frown lines, but she won't mind. Botox is not for her. Her face has character and she likes it that way. She believes that maintaining an alert state of mind is the most effective treatment to sharpen her bone structure and tone her facial muscles.

> More than beauty, what makes you lovable is the way you care for yourself.

The singular beauty of a woman is in the unique way she can brighten up a rainy day. In a city like Paris where the sky is often gray, women make it their business to stand out against the muted background of pale limestone and wet asphalt. The effort they put into looking good contributes to everyone's feeling more upbeat.

Maintaining one's appearance is not just an ego trip. In Paris, it is a form of public service—every woman's civic duty. Indeed, while sloppiness advertises that you don't care about what others think of you, paying attention to details is an expression of the respect you have for their judgment. By looking your best, you signal to everyone that their opinions matter.

Where I come from, a *jolie fille* (pretty girl) is like a ray of sunshine peeking through the clouds: wherever she goes, she brings a little joie de vivre to the multitude.

Why be an anonymous face in the crowd when you can be a bright spot in someone else's field of vision? The perfect arch of your eyebrows, the studied proportion of your jacket, or the subtle color scheme of your outfit—these are little gifts you can bestow on people around you.

Paint a picture for all of us art lovers out there.

Instead of merely trying to look good, ask yourself how you can help others feel good when they see you. Be gentle on their eyes. Give them something pleasant to focus on.

For instance, start with the color of your hair and build a palette around it. Blondes can accent their wardrobe with pale yellow and creamy beige, while partisans of the natural salt-and-pepper look can mix silvery tones with moody pastels such as gray-green and lavender.

If you prefer to work with contrasts, a scarf is the ultimate accessory. Its color can draw attention to that of your lipstick, your bag, or your earrings, with your clothes a mere background for those bright accents.

Or maybe your face is what you think will give others more pleasure. Then a white collar, a kerchief rolled around your neck, or a string of pearls will be the light-reflecting objects that will invite passersby to glance at you.

The way you care for yourself has a trickle-down effect on the people who cross your path each day. It's up to you to be worthy of their attention. Let beauty—your beauty—be a blessing to all who see you.

> Don't strive to be merely beautiful when you could be regal, adorable, marvelous, superb, captivating.

Appreciation of beauty depends on the words we use to describe it. We often fail to be moved by someone's exceptional appearance simply because our vocabulary is restricted. In English, there are twice as many words to describe ugliness as there are to describe beauty.

You would expect men, who spend so much time looking at women, to have at their disposal an endless supply of adjectives to describe the objects of their fascination. But that's not the case. In fact, men are often tongue-tied in the presence of members of the fair sex, preferring grunts to words to show their appreciation.

Strive to be regal, superb, captivating.

This is understandable. With so many beautiful women—and so little time—praising a woman is a daunting task. Men do their very best to honor the situation, but they cannot keep up with the ever-growing number of attractive women they encounter. You cannot blame a regular guy for being speechless in the presence of yet another person vested with unique qualities.

Let's face it, only a poet can do justice to the winsome figure of his son's girlfriend, the majestic stature of his mother-in-law, or the unfaltering smile of the girl who minds the coat check at his favorite restaurant.

So it's up to women to define beauty on their own terms. As much as I like the word *fabulous* to depict what's so distinctive about 51 percent of the world's population, I propose that we give it a rest. While we are at it, let's ban *pretty, lovely,* and *good-looking* when talking about each other. Instead, I would advocate we use terms like *ravishing, classic, indomitable,* or *gracious* in everyday conversation to characterize otherwise ineffable feminine attributes.

Or better yet, like the writer Dorothy Parker describing the dancer Isadora Duncan, let's turn beauty on its head with a rambunctious choice of words. "Here was a great woman," she wrote. "A magnificent, generous, gallant, reckless, fated fool of a woman. There was never a place for her in the ranks of the terrible, slow army of the cautious. She ran ahead, where there were no paths."

> Literature does as much for women
> as do beauty products.

Rare is the woman whose physical appeal is above and beyond a well-articulated compliment. Catherine Deneuve is a notable exception. For most Parisians, her inarguable beauty is the gold standard.

But unable to compete with someone so visibly accomplished, few women in my hometown are foolish enough to try to emulate the star of *Belle de Jour*. Whereas there are many celebrity look-alikes on the streets and in the malls in the United States, there are relatively few Deneuve wannabes on the boulevards of the French capital.

In fact, a typical Parisian will go out of her way to be different. She strives to be her extraordinary self—not quite "*belle*," but oh so unique.

If you want to be a femme fatale, smile with your mouth closed.

It's such a simple trick—and yet so seductive! Smile without parting your lips: get your eyes to sparkle rather than your teeth.

Smiling with your mouth closed is like repressing a discreet yawn: it makes your face tickle and your gaze watery. As a result you look slightly flushed and delicately misty. In contrast, baring your gums is an act of surrender that leaves little to the imagination.

Prettier than a full grin, the mysterious Mona Lisa smile illuminates your face from inside. Don't let the light escape by opening your mouth.

The most drastic makeovers are shifts in mental attitude. The way you think about beauty can transform the way you look. Become radiant by keeping an incandescent secret smoldering below the surface of all your facial expressions.

·10·

dieting
(THE SKINNY ON BLUBBER)

T H E other day, instead of splitting the lunch tab with a girl-friend, you impulsively declared: "Let me treat you!" A great meal sometimes causes us to express delight in ways that are fiscally injudicious.

Your friend raised her hand in protest.

"I insist!" you exclaimed.

Largesse is always a thrill, no matter how small. Unfortunately, the price we pay for having the means to share a bounty with others is not just monetary. A surplus always invites trouble.

"Fair enough," your friend said as you were giving your credit card to the waiter. "You pay for the meal, but let me buy dessert. How about a flourless chocolate cake à la mode and two spoons?"

See what I mean? Eight hundred and fifty calories later, you both waddled back to your respective offices. That afternoon, you almost fell asleep during a staff meeting and your friend could not concentrate on the proposal she was putting together for a big client.

An excess of satisfaction is often the source of unexpected disappointments.

At mealtime, whenever you cross the thin line that separates satisfaction from overgratification, your body goes into what diet experts call a "storage-only mode." Within minutes, insulin launches a stockpiling operation. You begin to feel sluggish as your metabolism slows down to allow your cells to quickly store excess calories as fat.

When you and I indulge our sweet tooth, our genes react according to an ancient Paleolithic blueprint designed to make the most of periods of abundance—so few and far apart twenty thousand years ago—by hoarding calories as fast as possible.

The next time you treat yourself or treat a friend, do so as discreetly as possible in order not to attract the attention of the ever-vigilant blubber manufacturers in your cells. Take small bites. Eat slowly. Breathe deeply. If you nibble quietly on your chocolate cake or your pumpkin-cranberry muffin, you might be able to get away with it without falling prey to the insulin trap.

You can try to trick your body chemistry by savoring rich foods leisurely.

Even though you may never be a victim of famine, nature keeps your calorie-stashing instincts in good working order, just in case. A signal from your brain that you are about to overindulge is enough to trigger a food-emergency practice run. Your metabolism reacts as if you were a ravenous hunter-gatherer.

All you need to do is absentmindedly reach for a bowl of roasted peanuts on the bar, or pile your plate high with pancakes, sausages, and eggs at one of those eat-as-much-as-you-want buffet brunches, and you will most likely experience a numbing sensation in your head similar to the strange buzz your television set emits when the government is testing the emergency broadcasting system.

*Take small bites. Don't invite the ravenous
blubber-devil in your cells.*

That mental buzz means that the "storage-only mode" has been activated. It's probably too late for you to do anything about it, so make the best of it. Dedicate the calories you are about to ingest (and the resulting blubber buildup) to your ancestors for whom a free-for-all was such a rare opportunity.

If you are worried about your weight, though, the next time you see a large buffet laden with mountains of tantalizing edibles, turn around and walk briskly in the opposite direction. Like secondhand smoke, secondhand supersizing puts your health at risk.

To reward yourself for leaving the gorging to others, every so often order half a portion of the most scrumptious thing on a menu. Don't expect a reduced tab, though: paying the full price for less food is in fact a bargain. When it minimizes your caloric intake, a restaurant is doing you a huge favor well worth a nice piece of change.

When you eat small amounts of rich food, you combine the pleasure of savoring tiny morsels with the mischievous satisfaction of outwitting an anachronistic program embedded in your genes.

> Paying more to eat less is counterintuitive, yet it is the smartest diet around.

Even more confusing to your body than the abundance of food is the abundance of health-related advice on the subject of nutrition. Diet books are just about as irresistible, and just about as addictive, as the fast food they denounce.

You cannot soothe a growling stomach with alarming words. In fact, cautionary dietary information is likely to unsettle your digestive system. Obsessive dieting only manages to activate the body's most basic biological assumption— that excessive concern about food can only stem from lack of nourishment. Before you know it, your genes have adjusted your metabolic rate and lowered your fat-burning thermostat, and you gain weight even if you eat less.

In other words, if you worry too much about what you put in your mouth, you send your body and your brain a malnutrition message that triggers its hoarding mechanism as surely as if you were a victim of hunger. Ironically, skipping meals, reading the small print on nutrition labels, counting calories, and scrutinizing your cholesterol levels actually increase the circumference of your waist.

Burn those diet books and learn to cook wholesome gourmet food instead.

Don't give up food, give up food phobia. Go on a diet of pleasant culinary thoughts. To that end, consider spending a little more time in the kitchen. The physical exertion alone will boost your energy level and help you keep your weight down. All things being equal, you probably get the same workout pacing in front of a stove as you do walking on a treadmill at the gym. Lifting heavy pots and pans can replace working out with free weights. And you can do your lunges and your squats while basting the roasted chicken or checking the progress of the ricotta-squash tart in the oven.

When you know how hard one has to exercise in order to lose weight, you'll realize that preparing balanced, non-fattening meals at home is well worth the effort, and a cinch in comparison. In terms of fitness benefits, an hour in the

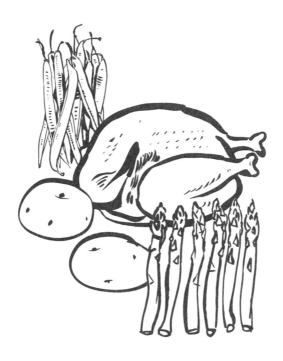

Go on a diet of pleasant culinary thoughts.

kitchen is on par with an hour at the gym. Yet, even though not eating out is the best way to keep a great figure or slim down from a size 14 to a size 10, very few dietitians ever urge their clients to open a cookbook and don an apron.

They cannot: in our culture, telling a woman to get back in the kitchen would be politically incorrect, even though today's cooks have it easy compared with their great-grandmothers. In the 1927 edition of her now-classic cookbook, the legendary French chef Madame Evelyn Saint-Ange instructs her readers to mix butter into mashed potatoes with vigorous strokes, so much so that their arms should still be sore an hour later! And she does sound like a drill sergeant when describing the proper way to beat egg whites (so firm they can support the weight of an egg in its shell) or pluck a still-warm, freshly killed chicken before trussing it for the oven.

Her muscular approach to cooking, not unusual in her day, is what has kept generations of French housewives in great physical shape. Ever wondered why Frenchwomen stay thin in spite of all that butter and foie gras? The answer I am about to give you is not going to make me popular with the fast-food lobbyists or with my girlfriends whose favorite kitchen appliance is their microwave oven.

Now you know: cooking—not dieting—is what Frenchwomen do to stay in shape.

You don't need to start a dish from scratch to make food healthier or easier on your stomach or your thighs. But what you must do is fire up your imagination as you fire up the stove, and stir up your nurturing instincts with as much love as you stir up the stewing contents of a heavy pot.

Learning to appease the yearning in your gut will feed more than your body: it will put you in touch with the intelligence of the organic world. Soon you will know instinctively when to bring a broth to a slow simmer and how to control the amount of evaporation in a steaming pan. You'll figure out on your own that it is best to refrain from stirring stewing apples to preserve their flavor. You might even be able to solve one of the greatest culinary mysteries of all time, namely how to keep potatoes piping hot while mashing them with butter.

There is more to food preparation than simply technique. Putting together a great meal is a creative act that requires both inspiration and mastery. Even the simplest gesture, like adding salt and pepper to a dish, demands that you combine panache with restraint, and flair with sound judgment.

A home-cooked meal is food for thought, a short essay on life written in the language of the senses.

• •

·11·

fashion

(PULLING YOURSELF TOGETHER)

THERE is, in the middle of our body, a Mason-Dixon Line that fashion designers call "the waist," around which our body supposedly articulates. If you ask me, nature did a pretty good job attaching two legs to a torso, but in the process of creating this engineering marvel that is our

Sometimes designers treat women as if they were
merely busts stuck on top of pedestals.

midriff, it left us with a no-man's-land separating north from south, the top from the bottom, the upper part of the body from what lies below.

Between these two regions, there is often what amounts to a sartorial civil war. The outfits we wear are frequently divided in two, each section with its own troops defending its turf against a potential invader. Up north, in Yankee territory, you find collars, necklines, armholes, sleeves, darts, buttons, lace, straps, and wires, while down south, among the Confederates, pleats, pockets, cuffs, zippers, and hems are holding the fort.

Season after season, designers come up with new strategies to maintain a semblance of peace between these two warring factions, with the line between the two camps being redrawn from time to time. The elusive waist moves up and down, creeping all the way up the rib cage or slipping down past the hips toward the thighs.

More than a physical reality (just look around: how many of us have an hourglass figure?), the waist is a symbolic line we draw halfway across the body to convince ourselves that the higher and lower parts of our nature can be managed separately. While subscribing to this dualistic view of the universe, fashion struggles with it. Sometimes the vogue is to cinch the middle of outfits in such a way as to give the impression that women are merely busts stuck on top of pedestals, but at other times the latest styles celebrate a fluid and seamless silhouette, blurring the very line that was so critical the previous year.

> Don't think of yourself as a top and a bottom. Use fashion as a way to reconcile what's above with what's below.

A disastrous outcome of this sartorial bipolarization is the now widespread tendency among women to consider their body as the sum of its parts. "If only I had bigger breasts," complains a reed-thin creature. "I don't like my sloping shoulders," your subadolescent daughter is likely to announce one day out of the blue. And, to be honest, haven't you already noticed the annoying way the skin on the pointy tip of your elbow has a tendency to droop?

If we can name a bit of flesh, we will find a reason to be dissatisfied with it.

Only safe from our criticisms are fragments that can't be described easily. No one so far has ever found fault with the piece of skin between her thumb and index finger or with the connection between her ears and her upper jaw, though I am sure that plastic surgeons will soon convince us to add these neglected areas to the list of our concerns.

Fashion is a nonsurgical alternative to correct what we believe to be our imperfections, with designers nipping and tucking fabric, leather, and fur instead of muscles and tissues. And how much more fun is their methodology! Season after season, the likes of Karl Lagerfeld, Oscar de la Renta, Christian Lacroix, and Jean-Paul Gaultier have been able to create rollicking collections that not only capture the spirit of fun but also reinvent it systematically.

So, in spite of the fact that fashion is a tyrannical presence in our lives, we can't help but be tantalized as we hunt for that perfectly divine outfit that will not only hide our many physical flaws but do so lightheartedly.

As much as we may hate to admit it, the frivolous and capricious nature of fashion is its most valuable characteristic, its vagaries the thing that helps us shrug off our ever-encroaching dissatisfaction with ourselves with that airy sense of humor the French call *désinvolture*.

One should never attempt to eliminate the element of trial and error inherent to fashion: its soul-searching dimension is its very raison d'être. Time-saving practices such as online shopping or ordering clothes from a catalog reduce fashion to an endeavor of stultifying practicality that celebrates the mundane over the festive.

Beware: standard-issue civilian clothes are the next thing, unless we remember that the goal of fashion is to "release us from the banality of the world," to quote Diana Vreeland, the legendary editor of *Vogue*. And indeed, there is a little less joy in the universe when fashion advice turns into mere shopping information.

> Fashion is more than great clothes:
> it's a way to dress that pokes
> fun at our lame discontentment.

In your lifetime, in your search for the look that says "Wow, it's me!" you have probably purchased black pants by the hundreds, dozens of jeans, countless khakis, umpteen jackets, so many knit tops it makes you dizzy just thinking about them, and eight really nice suits. If you had to name six of your most memorable outfits, though, five of them would be dresses.

We love dresses: they make us feel tall and streamlined—a fully integrated being, the same person from neck to knees, with no breach or bulge in between.

A woman wearing a dress looks "pulled together." Somehow, she seems more polished, respectable, noble—even more saintly—than a woman wearing an outfit that gives her easy access to her belly button. While the devil cuts a dashing figure in a three-piece suit by Ralph Lauren (or Prada), we picture God in heaven flaunting his almightiness in a long, flowing shift by Eileen Fisher.

In the rearview mirror of time, a dress is cut out of the fabric of life. The memory of your pale green jersey dress will forever summon the magical moment when you strolled barefoot at dusk on the beach in Puerto Rico with a cute stranger who you knew would become your better half.

The thought of your spaghetti-strap, bias-cut silk slip will take you right back to the day you had drinks with your dad and his new wife at the Plaza Hotel and to the sense of loss you experienced afterward.

Meanwhile, still hanging in your closet, waiting to be fashionable again, is your fabulous tweed jumper—very Audrey Hepburn when paired with a black turtleneck and big sunglasses—the gamine style for all ages.

Though we go through everyday life in separates, switching tops and bottoms to accommodate our changing moods (and our changing sizes), we associate extraordinary circumstances with dresses. Graduations, weddings, anniversaries, funerals—and taking an out-of-town client to dinner on a weeknight—are as many occasions on which to roll out the red carpet and wear something slinky that hugs your body in all the right places and smooths your curves like a virtual girdle.

> Always keep at least one fabulous dress in your closet: it is the gold standard against which you measure everything else you wear.

The ultimate allegory for happiness is probably the sight of a girl twirling in a dress. The famous movie poster of *The Sound of Music* comes close to capturing this elusive feeling. If, instead of a girlish pinafore frock, Julie Andrews had been wearing a pair of jeans with a shirt, chances are the poster would not have had the same universal appeal.

No picture of a woman in separates could ever convey the same lighthearted elation. There is always something slightly fastidious about a composite silhouette, even when the pieces are casually thrown together.

And sure enough, it takes advanced problem-solving skills to successfully coordinate a wardrobe of separates. Though tops and bottoms are supposedly more versatile than complete outfits, putting them together is aesthetically challenging. Like the pieces of a puzzle, only the right tops and bottoms will latch together with that deeply satisfying snap.

I hate to contradict fashion stylists, but there are only a couple of ways to wear a particular blazer, cardigan, or skirt.

*A perfectly divine outfit lifts your spirits
and enhances your sense of humor.*

Even though showing readers how to mix and match the same two tops and bottoms to create twelve completely different outfits is a foolproof formula for playful magazine layouts, in real life the exercise is unnerving and laborious.

Think of your tops and bottoms as fashion items separated at birth.

In most closets, blouses, camisoles, shells, and T-shirts are segregated from slacks and skirts. Why not reunite the most likely pairs on the same hanger? It would be the smart thing to do to avoid the tactical nightmare of dressing in the morning. No longer a jumble, the content of your wardrobe would then be a collection of ready-to-wear outfits, each with a personality of its own.

What stops most of us from doing this is the assumption that it is unbecoming to wear the same combination of clothes repeatedly. Confusing fashion with newness, we assume that the latest looks have more style than the looks of previous seasons. Sadly enough, we are often right because so many of our favorite garments that looked flattering at first have turned into rags after just a couple of wearings or washes.

The short shelf life of low-priced clothing forces you and me to keep buying new outfits. Frenchwomen, who typically own half as many articles of clothing as the average American woman, operate under a different set of rules. They believe in spending more money for quality clothes and limiting their choices to a few tried-and-true combinations. They secure a look for themselves with only a handful of well-loved garments that they wear repeatedly with flair and poise. Familiarity with each item is what gives them the self-confidence to create a personal style tailored to fit their specific body type.

Elegance is not what you wear but how graceful you feel when you wear it.

Even when she shows up in the most improbable getup (a summer dress under a ski jacket, a classic raincoat lined with pink fake fur, cargo pants, and high heels), the Frenchwoman never gives the impression of sporting a costume. In fact, she wears all her clothes with the same panache with which she wears her scarves: a desultory elegance that's hers and hers alone.

Like slipping effortlessly into a favorite outfit, tying a scarf for her is an act of reconciliation between what's above and what's below. With a rakish kerchief tied around her neck, she somehow feels more together, with her head secured on her shoulders.

Don't just take my word for it: whenever you need a fashion fix, add a scarf to your outfit. The perkier the better. For a jaunty variation on the French "loop," take a classic silk square, fold it crosswise into a triangle, and twirl it into a rolled-up horizontal band. Without further ado, grab the middle of the band and fold it in half. Wrap this loop around your neck, insert the loose ends of the scarf into the noose, rotate sideways and tighten. Voilà.

Tying a scarf is the equivalent of a full fashion makeover—French style.

> *Fashion* is a noun but also a verb: to fashion means to carve, sculpt, and shape by hand.

Fashion works through the sense of touch as much as through sight. To guide your sartorial choices, let tactile impressions make the difference.

Fashion rhymes with action.

Fluidity and resilience are two essential qualities of a great-looking garment. So pick clothes for their texture more than their shape or color. Never wear anything that scratches or is too tight when you bend yet too loose when you sit down. For the same reason, stay away from garments with a stiff, glued-in lining that does not move with the body, seams that pucker and crawl like hairy caterpillars, and anything whose label is stitched in place with thorny nylon threads.

The soft brush of a hem against your calves, the characteristic sound of silk as your fingernails skim its luscious surface, the kiss of a collar on the back of your neck, the gentle pressure of a bustier around your rib cage—these are the telltale signs of fashionable clothes.

Think of fashion not as a look but as what happens to your body and mind when you slip into a cashmere cardigan so fine it weighs less than a spoonful of sugar, step into a draped silk jersey dress as sensual as a shiver, or loll around in pajamas as lustrous as pearls in white sand.

• •

Shopping
(A GUILT-FREE GUIDE TO RECKLESS SPLURGING)

T H E next time you stand at the checkout counter, relish that fleeting nanosecond between the moment when you've laid out your money and the moment when the drawer of the cash register opens to welcome your donation. It's an emotionally charged interval, like releasing into the wild an animal born in captivity. After a brief hesitation, your hard-earned dollars spring forward to join other dollars in the free-market jungle where they belong.

On that account, never feel guilty again when reaching deep inside your purse and pulling out your credit card. Your next purchase is yet another gift to the universe, a selfless gesture of sorts, an act that benefits others probably more than it benefits you!

We often spend money freely in order to experience the joy of passing it along. Contrary to what some moralists would like us to believe, acquisitiveness is not always the main motive when we go on a shopping spree. The goods we get in exchange for what we pay are only a small portion of the full value of a transaction. A chance to put money back into the economy and give it to deserving people or causes is in fact an important part of the equation.

Let me refresh the memory of those among us who insist that we are a nation of greedy shoppers. Can you remember how you felt the last time you bought overpriced lemonade and cookies from a seven-year-old sidewalk vendor? Or how proud you were when you got a painting directly from an unknown artist and paid fair market value for it? Or how good it felt to buy a favorite niece a quaint dollhouse made of wood by a local craftsman instead of a plastic one with a clock tower and a three-door garage?

Admit it: shopping is often a conduit for some of your most enlightened and generous impulses.

We go shopping in order to get what money can't buy:
wisdom, common sense, insight.

Buying stuff is a way to invest in the things we value and support the people who profit from it.

Why not think of shopping as an altruistic venture, even when you are splurging on a fifth pair of strappy heels you can't afford or upgrading your cell phone for the latest model with a bejeweled cover? The stuff we take home in shopping bags is merely a token of appreciation from retailers for investing a portion of our income in their enterprise!

Reckless consumption has gotten a bad name for itself recently, yet the way people spend their disposable income and the choices they make once they are in a store shape their future and the future of others as much as if not more than the way they vote.

In the big picture, assessing one's wealth by measuring one's net worth is shortsighted. What makes you rich is not how much you keep but how much you can afford to spend on things that are useless or superfluous!

Today, there is too much talk about the benefits of increasing one's worth and not enough about the value—and the pleasures—of decreasing it. When was the last time someone got on TV to explain to you why it's important to let cash slip through your fingers? How to stop worrying about bad investments? And how to best dispatch money into the blue yonder?

To compensate for this critical lack of information, here are a few pointers:

Rediscover the pleasure of paying cash.

There is a time in everyone's life when spending five dollars is a thrill. Today, you probably would have to multiply this amount by a hundred or a thousand and apply it toward a single purchase to feel as insanely rich as when you were six and you proudly lined up a handful of quarters from your piggy bank to buy pink lipstick.

More than the amount of money you spend, it is the deliberate way you spend it that defines how affluent you feel. Laying crisp dollar bills on a counter, for instance, is a lot more meaningful than scribbling one's signature at the bottom of a small piece of paper as curly as an onion peel.

Almost anachronistic today, handling dollar bills and writing checks are gestures that still preserve something of the interpersonal dimension of a commercial transaction. In contrast, debit cards dehumanize what used to be a transfer of funds from one person to the other—from customer to shopkeeper.

But the big spender in you is safe and sound as long as you still have loose change in your pocket. Even though handsome gold coins are a thing of the past, quarters, nickels, and dimes are still some of the most beautiful objects we carry around. Though we tend to forget that they are delicate pieces of jewelry in the palm of our hand, they can act as a reminder that spending money is an aesthetically charged endeavor.

One can feel richer—and have a richer inner life—simply by taking the time to hunt for exact change when buying the little things that make being alive so pleasurable. You don't want to punch in a PIN or sweep a plastic card in front of an electric eye to get something as special as individually wrapped chocolates, for instance, or birthday candles, or padded satin hangers. Make money go a little further by counting pennies when buying pistachio oil, commemorative stamps, embroidered Chinese slippers, fresh figs, local road maps, spiral-bound notebooks, black-and-white postcards, sourdough bread, wicker baskets, and almond croissants.

Make small purchases count as much as big ones.

If you become aware of the way banknotes and coins wiggle their way out of your purse and into the system, you will develop what is commonly called "taste"—an ability to judge the quality of things independently of their price.

Lo and behold, you will become choosy with strawberries, only buying them when they are in season.

You'll discover that in fact you prefer ordinary toothbrushes to fancy ones.

You'll be willing to spend a small fortune on a very good pair of scissors to trim your bangs between $180 visits to your hairstylist.

You'll use white vinegar as a household cleaner and water softener.

You'll cook with butter and bake with lard (a very small amount goes a long way).

You'll buy your crockery from a friend who is a potter.

And you'll be the first to discover the trendy new kitchen supply store at the local mall, where you will buy an authentic Provençal oilcloth *toile cirée* for the breakfast table.

If you have a wholesome one-on-one relationship with what money can buy, chances are you'll be able to get what money *can't* buy: wisdom, common sense, insight. Exercising your judgment with small purchases will turn out to be good practice for making major ones. If you take the time to give merchants exact change, you will be ready on the day you become the beneficiary of a modest inheritance or receive an unexpected bonus. No one will be surprised to learn that you bought a small farmhouse in Picardy, went back to school to get a degree in pharmacy, or financed a fifteen-minute documentary film.

Look for a "steal"—but do not cheat yourself.

Each of us is a potential barbarian at the gate; we love to rummage through bins, racks, and piles of merchandise. No wonder: for millennia, the best way to legitimately acquire valuables was to steal them. In the time of Homer, wars were seen as the occasion of much plundering and looting, with the booty the rightful reward of soldiers.

Today, getting something for nothing is still a shopper's

Buy your crockery from a friend who is a potter.

fantasy. We approach a major spree with ancient blood coursing through our veins. The prospect of a "steal" is so powerful that only intense physical efforts, acute danger, extreme novelty, and unbearable suspense can deliver the same immediacy, the same eagerness, the same sense of being recklessly alive as a private, one-day-only Hermès sample sale. Holding the engraved invitation in your hand triggers a trancelike state similar to that of being enthralled by the thundering drumroll of a military marching band.

Paradoxically, though, a "steal" is a sure way to get robbed. Hermès notwithstanding, the majority of so-called sample sales, bargain basements, going-out-of-business sales, and designer outlets are cleverly disguised venues for retailers to get rid of frumpy, shoddy, or ill-gotten merchandise.

What's more—more detrimental to your soul, anyway—is the way you cheat yourself of the pleasure of appreciating the work of others. A passion for markdowns could deprive you of the opportunity to support the effort and talent of the men and women who still fabricate and handle some of the most beautiful things on earth.

> Commerce is not about impersonal greed;
> it's about human relationships.

More hunters than gatherers, we enter a store cautiously, our senses on alert, scoping the place for opportunities and dangers. A deceptively friendly "May I help you?" coming from the cavernous back of the room gives us the jitters. The most challenging part of shopping is behaving gracefully in the presence of shopkeepers and sales associates.

Civilization began when fierce invaders curbed their territorial ambition long enough to learn to negotiate with the local tradesmen of the countries they were occupying. They stopped being barbarians and became denizens by interacting daily, as we do, with opinionated merchants, intimidating boutique owners, overobliging attendants, cool-looking cashiers, and cranky little old ladies behind counters.

American tourists traveling abroad are sometimes made to feel like invaders when they are chastised by local shopkeepers for not greeting a salesperson personably before asking for an item, inspecting the merchandise carefully before

Chances are, in the last hour, you've said "thank you," "please," and "you're welcome" at least a dozen times.

deciding whether or not to buy it, asking for its price aloud, or chatting on a cell phone while paying the bill.

We often measure our degree of sophistication—and the degree of sophistication of others—by the way we handle ourselves in stores. Miss Manners, for instance, suggests shoppers call a woman waiting on them "miss," regardless of her age, while expecting to be called "madam" in return. Other, less arcane courtesy rules include never expressing your opinion about an article someone else is purchasing and being careful not to crowd the counter or block the entrance door. Etiquette maven Charlotte Ford goes even further by advising her readers to write a complimentary letter about an exemplary salesgirl to the head of the department.

> The most valuable transaction in a commercial situation is an exchange of good manners.

Look at the goods you bring back home as certificates of gentility. In the last hour or so, you've been gracious, patient, friendly. You've said "thank you," "please," and "you're welcome" at least a dozen times. You've demonstrated kindness, respect, consideration, and honesty.

We go to stores and pay good money for things we don't need in order to satisfy our selfless needs as social beings.

• •

entertaining
(PROMOTING CIVILIZATION AT HOME)

I T usually happens toward the beginning of the second hour of a party. For no apparent reason, the decibel level in your living room goes from fizzle to sizzle in less than a minute. There is a buzz in the air and laughter in the distance. It is the turning point, the moment you have been waiting for.

The guest of honor at all gatherings,
conviviality is often late to the party.

Paradoxically, rollicking good times make a quiet entrance. By the time your guests are ready to have fun, there is no longer a crush around the buffet table—you can retire what remains of the baked ham to the kitchen—and fewer people are rummaging through half-emptied bottles for that third refill. The scented candles on the mantelpiece have melted down to puddles of liquid gold, and no one is watching the tennis game on TV any longer, its flickering image petering out like an unattended fire in the fireplace.

At long last you can relax. Your party needs no more prodding—it has acquired a levity of its own.

While an hour ago, at the beginning of the soiree, your famished guests were worried about the clothes they wore, the price of oil, the inverted yield curve, and the design of their websites, they are now surprisingly poised.

Satiated at last, sitting back in their chairs or comfortably slumped on your sofa, pressing flesh in the hallway or leaning casually against a wall, each of them is a study in quiet joviality.

The women look twice as pretty as they did when they walked in. Their cheeks are now glossy; no longer powdered, their noses are satiny; and only the barest trace of crimson is left on their shiny lips. Huddled in a corner, four of them are comparing notes on the cosmetic procedure du jour, their peals of laughter, their pouts, and their frowns proof positive that Botox is not as widely used as one might fear.

In a corner, the collage artist who lives next door is discussing the health benefits of aspirin with the shy foreign exchange student you invited at the last minute, while center stage someone whose name you can't remember regales everyone within earshot with the unsolved mystery of the five-hundred-year-old corpses found in the crypt of the Medicis.

Tomorrow morning your guests will wake up to find out that their favorite jacket is not back from the dry cleaner, that the day promises to be unseasonably cold, and that they forgot to buy milk for breakfast, but right now they are immune from such petty concerns.

They are your guests, a breed apart, members of a civilized tribe for whom the most enjoyable form of entertainment is still a lively conversation.

> Invite interesting strangers to your
> parties: give them a pleasant opportunity
> to forgo self-involvement.

A successful party is one during which a roomful of strangers, with no particular connection with one another, let go of their narcissistic preoccupations long enough to become unexpectedly interested in one another. In an ideal world, even before they cross your threshold, your guests should feel curious about the people they will meet around your buffet table.

To this end, spice up your parties with a sense of trepidation by encouraging your guests to imagine, mingling among them, enigmatic people whose real identity they can only surmise. A little trickery may be necessary. For instance, tell everyone that the party is given in honor of an out-of-town friend whose professional accomplishments you will extol, but in the vaguest possible terms. Or enroll your friends in an innocent cover-up operation: let it slip that the evening is a pretext to introduce two very good people to each other—though you can't reveal their names. Or, if you are single, confide to your guests that you have invited someone you have a crush on—big-time—and that you will probably be a wreck.

In other words, give your guests the impression that they are on the inside track. You want them to scan the room as they come in, wondering whether the unassertive-looking gent is the big-name architect recently interviewed by Charlie Rose, which of the twin sisters sitting on the window seat owns a fast-growing bicycle-rental franchise, and if the man offering them a drink is the swoonworthy fellow you told them about.

Neither costume parties nor masked balls, your get-togethers can nonetheless be the occasion for some playful speculation.

Parties are most enjoyable when the people who just shared food and wine are not sharing their complete biography as well. The French, whose literary salons were renowned for

*It's all about making your guests feel
that they are special.*

their wit and repartee, and whose legendary sense of fun is showing no sign of abating, frown upon too much candor in social situations. Talking about yourself is in poor taste, they believe, not because it is a sign of conceit, but because it spoils the pleasure of the person at the receiving end of your revelations. The less one knows about someone, the more intriguing the encounter and the more entertaining the possibilities.

You cannot prevent people from talking about themselves, but, as either a hostess or a guest, you can advance civilization by changing the topic of conversation whenever someone is about to release socioeconomic data about himself.

Go ahead: interrupt bloody bores by recounting how you were abducted by aliens.

The paranormal and the occult are instant curiosity boosters. Mention something out of the ordinary that happened to you recently, and everyone in the room will want to share a similar anecdote. Also keep in mind that incredible stories about pets who saved the lives of their masters, home-improvement debacles, and how to sell old jewelry are foolproof crowd-pleasers.

Other civilized topics of conversation between partygoers include peeling versus washing mushrooms; the thriving art scene in Houston, Texas; philosophically vexing conundrums; songbirds of New England; drip-hose garden technology; the dubious mores of the day; whether brown is the new black; walnut cake recipes; the advantages of the metric system; the popularity of graphic novels; and the comparative merits of the Oxford and Webster's dictionaries.

> Some people should not be invited together: babies, real estate agents, and anyone who is either lactose intolerant or recently engaged.

Some of your sweetest and dearest friends are party poopers and should be invited separately, when you can lavish all your attention on them. For instance, do not impose on your guests globe-trotters who are just back from an exotic trip abroad—stories about Mayan ruins, giant turtles, and Arctic Circle yachting lose their appeal when transplanted to living rooms. For similar reasons, don't invite new parents who only want to talk about their kid, more than two singles of the same sexual persuasion, or your boss, your landlord, and the secretary of your co-op board.

In other words, don't invite high-maintenance killjoys. Though the word *entertaining* suggests that the perfect host should be able to tap-dance across the living room floor, twirl batons, tell jokes, and make the rounds to share his or her wit with everyone, it is not the case. A soiree is not a reelection campaign. You don't have to get everyone's vote in order to fulfill your social engagement. What you need to do, though, is give every single one of your guests a magic moment to take away.

Throw a party: conjure up a world more perfect than the one in which we will wake up tomorrow morning.

In the annals of revelry, the most extravagantly choreographed fetes all had a sleepwalking quality, as if to prolong a dreamlike illusion as long as possible. Legendary hosts from Louis XIV to Martha Stewart have spared no expense to enhance the pleasure of their guests with phantasmagoric contraptions: they have created palaces made entirely of marzipan and candies; hung mirrored chandeliers in the form of castles from tall trees; fit a full orchestra inside enormous cakes; engulfed revelers in a deluge of rose petals; trained lions to dance and even sing; and convinced leopards to ride on top of leaping unicorns.

But all you and I need to do to replicate the same feat is treat our guests as if they were all mysterious visitors from some faraway realms. Or, to quote the Hebrews of the Old Testament: "Do not forget to entertain strangers, for by so doing some people have entertained angels unexpectedly."

• •

·14·

love

(HOW TO LOSE YOUR HEAD)

BACK from a business lunch with a man whose case she was handling, a young lawyer went to her office, closed the door, and gently banged her head against the wall, moaning. She had a crush on her client! Though she was mortified, she felt alive, more so than she had in a long time. Whatever amorous torments lay ahead, she decided, they were preferable to the false sense of equanimity that had been hers the day before.

Falling in love is a sweet malady, and probably the only illness we suffer joyfully.

At first, infatuation manifests itself as a physiological event with physical consequences not unlike hypoglycemia, or maybe the onset of flu. Only later do you realize that what ails you is not a passing malaise but something else altogether, something improbably tender and violent, the first symptoms of this catastrophic disorder we call love.

And indeed, months later, well into an unethical affair she kept secret from even her best friend, the lawyer's condition was still deliciously desperate. The daily muffled phone conversations with her lover had the same effect on her as their clandestine lovemaking. The sound of his voice would flood her body with chemicals and leave her short of breath, her heart beating, her head spinning, with shivers coursing from the inside of her knees to the tip of her elbows.

Why do I love him? you wonder. You love him because anyone whose presence makes you feel alive deserves your total devotion.

If, in her wretched condition, she were offered an instant cure, would she take the antidote and forget the whole thing? My guess is that given a choice, very few people would forgo the experience of being swept off their feet—even though it means drowning in a brew of conflicting emotions.

But when it comes to love, it's not up to us to decide. The

minute we are bewitched by this bizarre condition, we have no choice but to go along for the ride. Trying to figure out whether the lucky guy is worth the trouble is futile—Cupid never reveals his master plan.

Love is the answer, they say. What no one tells you is that you are left wrestling with the question What do I love most, the object of my rueful affection or the irrepressible euphoria that's mine as a result of some stultifying hormonal collusion? And what came first, my emotions or my feelings, my heart or my head, my cells or my neurons?

Not knowing for sure drives you crazy, but you are ready to put up with the major inconvenience of being temporarily insane in order to find out.

The suspense could kill you. The fact that it doesn't is one of life's greatest mysteries. Meanwhile, either consumed by blissful thoughts or assailed by injured feelings—or both—you cannot begin to measure the profound transformation that is taking place in you.

Oh, benevolent Mother Nature, who invented love as a motive for personal growth! Under the pretext of loving someone else, she cajoles us into loving the person we happen to be.

Like water carving canyons into the earth, romantic daydreaming carves deep valleys into our soul. As epochal as geologic time—and as excruciatingly slow—the hours spent waiting to be reunited with a loved one are transforming our inner landscape by eroding the primitive rock formations of our ego.

So give in—love him unconditionally: it's
not even about him, it's about you.

Through a veil of warm tears, life oftentimes looks improbably beautiful. A marvelous sense of doom is likely to interrupt our most woeful ruminations—even as we hanker and pine for someone whose absence we mourn.

There is a strange comfort in being able to feel fortunate

*When you are in love, the world
looks improbably beautiful.*

in spite of the grief. Ah, to be vulnerable, and yet at the same time to be smart, funny, silly, tough, and insightful!

How could you be so insensitive before as not to behold the trivial splendor of ordinary things? you wonder. Whereas you used to be somewhat discontented with your fate, you now feel ridiculously lucky because you noticed, as if for the first time, the elegant tracery of ivy on a brick wall or the tiny blossoms of weeds pushing through cracks in the sidewalk.

And there is more in store for you as time goes by and you find solace in your melancholy: not only are you more likely now to see greatness in what you used to call mediocrity, you also discover the beauty of operatic music, turn up at poetry readings, find older men more attractive, are less critical of your mother's taste in clothes, develop a preference for Côtes du Rhône wines over Bordeaux, and reach out to friends you had neglected. But you derive the greatest pleasure from knowing that you can now feel pain and yet give love in return.

> Loving him translates into loving yourself—
> loving the love that burns inside your chest.

Give in to love and eventually you become your own best friend. In due course, the time you spend alone with yourself is as precious to you as the time you spend alone with the one you love.

It is a paradox, and yet it only makes you love him more. He has given you the greatest gift of all: days filled with won-

Her lust for him soon turns into lust for life.

der, and nights, too. Lo and behold, you've turned into the kind of woman who welcomes insomnia as she would the impromptu visit of her lover in the middle of the night.

To your own surprise, you grow fond of the wee hours,

those timeless moments when you can move silently in the dark, caressing corners and angles as you negotiate your way to the kitchen to pour yourself a glass of cold water and stare quizzically at the dispassionate face of the wall clock.

> Falling in love with a man is only a prelude to falling in love with life.

As a transformative experience, falling madly in love is on a par with pregnancy and childbirth, surviving a major earthquake, winning a million-dollar lottery, hiring an architect to design your dream house, buying a Van Gogh, saving somebody's life, learning to play the piano as an adult, adopting an infant, and living long enough to attend the wedding of a grandchild.

Only in hindsight do we find out what this emotional upheaval was all about: when the chemical storm recedes—when deep affection keeps company with smoldering passion—you have a new job, a better marriage, a larger apartment, or a more realistic understanding of who you are and what you need.

Yet, even though it is probably the most common of all life's miracles, momentarily losing one's head is nonetheless a lonely endeavor. Infatuation is one of the few instances when forewarned is not forearmed. The experience of others turns out to be of no use to you when you find yourself in a similar situation.

Ironically, you are on your own the minute his lips touch yours. What you are getting into is not a relationship—not yet. The first kiss is the beginning of a solo adventure, a journey you must undertake alone.

Love will take you by surprise, unless you prepare for it with a few surprises of your own.

Rather than be taken aback when your senses take leave of your reason, give your impulsive heart a couple of unexpected lessons. Venture away from safe assumptions. In fact, get into the habit of greeting minor delays and setbacks playfully, as training exercises for future romance.

In your most besotted state, you will remember to lighten up if you have practiced a little mischievousness beforehand.

Consider yourself lucky if you are the kind of person who is accident-prone—who, for example, drops drinks, chips china, crashes into mirrors, and arrives a day late to dinner parties: you can probably get through a devastating love affair with your dignity intact. Accustomed as you are to your own foolish behavior, you will be able to keep your sense of humor in the darkest hours of your *affaire de cœur*.

But those among us who are less likely to hit their fingers with a hammer or forget where the car is parked will have to work harder to find the blithe spirit necessary to overcome the hurdles they are sure to encounter in the pursuit of their most ardent hopes and suave ambitions.

*Falling in love triggers the same adrenaline rush
as watching objects plummet in free fall.*

Learn not to take yourself too seriously, if you can. Comparable to zero gravity in the brain, an ability to be silly is the next best thing to the weightlessness endured by astronauts in outer space. According to NASA scientists, episodes of light-headedness slow down our perception of time and make us less likely to feel pain—two valuable assets for lovers engaged in a passionate brawl with their senses.

To lose one's head is to release one's heart and experience a moment of inane levity.

Only this morning, while fumbling to open your umbrella, you dropped your bag, parts of its contents spilling on the wet sidewalk. Did you feel annoyed? Not at first. If you think back carefully, you will recall that, at the very moment it happened, before your bag hit the ground, you experienced the delicious vertigo of a fleeting loss of control.

Falling in love triggers the same adrenaline rush as watching objects plummet in free fall.

Just as beneficial as dropping things is misplacing them. Remember the last time you thought you lost your cell phone—or maybe someone stole it—and you drove yourself crazy until you eventually found it in the pocket of your bathrobe? Again, recall what you felt when your fingers identified the lost item: it was as heady a sensation as the brief queasiness that's yours when the plane in which you are strapped lifts off the runway and rises effortlessly into the clouds.

Being swept off your feet is not unlike breathing a sigh of relief as you are set free—free from pettiness, from worry, or from gravity. Indeed, it is with wings on your heels that you run to your amorous rendezvous—a woman airborne, traveling with the wind toward self-realization.

• •

family
(KEYS TO GENERATIONAL ROAD MAPS)

IN almost every family, there is a little girl who is pure joy.
Whenever her aunts, uncles, cousins, or grandparents lay
eyes on her, they are reminded of how lucky they are to be
related to her—and to each other.

You peer at her discreetly as she plays with her stuffed animals or daydreams in front of her plate. You are careful not to stare directly at her: it would be like looking at the sun during an eclipse, so intense is the inner light behind her innocent features. Sometimes you wonder why more grown-ups do not wear sunglasses when they are around kids: one could damage one's sight gaping at these luminous creatures.

Why do some girls between the ages of two and seven have the gift of making their relatives feel joy? I don't know. Often it has to do with their looks, but it could also be their intelligence, their gentleness, or, on the contrary, their drive, their pluck, or their fearless curiosity. It doesn't have much to do with blood ties: these gamines can be adopted or brought into the fold as stepchildren. Possibly, the reason they have this effect on adults has to do with the structure of our brain. Chances are, we are hardwired to see in some girls (future mothers of generations to come) all the potential we wish for ourselves and our offspring, and we project our yearning onto them.

Meanwhile, something about them is so genuine, no one is immune to their charm, except their parents and siblings, who are usually too busy to appreciate their uncanny ability to delight people. This is a good thing: if the girls were spoiled, they would have to relinquish their role as family catalysts to some other little ingenues.

Nothing in life quite compares to the joy of finding intact in one innocent child a piece of the unfathomable puzzle that is the destiny of the human race. The fleeting sense of grace her presence elicits is as inscrutable as one of those cryptic mathematical formulas that attempt to plumb the mystery of the universe. But how can a mystery be hidden, unknowable, and yet keen on dolls, party clothes, and white kittens?

> A family is a tribe whose members look
> quizzically at each other and
> wonder: "Where do I come from?"

Family trees grow vertically, but what gives them character are their transversal limbs. When people of the same tribe congregate, they branch out diagonally, reaching thwartwise for each other to form cursory, unpremeditated alliances.

When no magic little girl happens to be around to make you feel special (eventually, they do grow up to become typical preteens), other members of the family fill the gap. You discover some unexpected fondness for a former mother-in-law, the sister of your dad, or a nephew who grew up in Australia but whose parents recently moved nearby.

You may develop something like a friendship with unlikely members of your extended family. More than saying grace before a meal or sharing reminiscences around a fireplace, what makes family get-togethers gratifying are those impromptu conspiratorial glances firing across generational divides, past the confines of the nuclear family, to the far side of the kindred galaxy.

Almost unnoticed, seldom acknowledged, these brief moments of empathy between near strangers are at the heart of warm and fuzzy family feelings. They lift your spirits, even though they last less than a second, like that quick look of amusement an aunt and her niece might exchange while a third cousin brags about a grossly lucrative real estate deal, or the pleasant surprise caused by the spontaneous offer to empty the dishwasher from your brother's new stepdaughter.

Relatives who command the most attention are seldom the ones who make family gatherings memorable.

A pretty sister or a wealthy son-in-law, though they get the most accolades, do not bring as much to the party as eccentrics and oddballs. Would your family be as much fun without your endlessly politically correct brother (such a sweetheart, but what a bore!); your sultry niece, who, at the young age of twenty-five, is already twice-divorced; and your widowed mother-in-law whose gambling habit raises eyebrows?

In every family, even the runt of the litter is someone's favorite relative and the black sheep is never without a first cousin once removed who secretly admires him.

No matter how unpopular you think you may be at times with your next of kin (maybe you decided to become a physical therapist instead of a doctor), rest assured that there is

In almost every family, there is a little girl
who is pure joy.

someone out there of the same ilk and stripe who has a soft spot for you.

Trying to garner the love and respect of your kissing kin by tooting your horn is counterproductive. Telling them that you were awarded a gold medal by the Society of Publications Designers is not going to do the trick, either. You may elicit their flattery but not win their affection. Don't try to cajole a little old lady who equates marriage with happiness or impress a snotty nephew whose most prized possession is a battered snowboard.

Your relatives don't need to know that you are a smart hedge fund manager, a talented musician, or a brilliant advertising executive. Keep your stellar professional achievements to yourself. Try to fit in rather than stand out.

Your family is a shelter where you can go and hide when you are tired of being fabulous in the outside world.

Your happiest childhood memories often involve hectic holiday celebrations, when grown-ups were too busy to pay attention to you and you could disappear with your cousins in the attic or the rec room to play endless games with them. Back then, going unnoticed for a couple of hours was a form of bliss, a relief from having to be Daddy's pride and joy or Mommy's little darling.

Going unnoticed today can still be a source of sweet satisfaction: family gatherings are not class reunions. Rather than try to shine among your peers, it is more fun and less taxing to connect with the younger generations.

Experience the joy of being able to cuddle with a drooling, wiggling, six-month-old baby wearing tiny pearl earrings who everyone says looks just like you. To get all dressed up to go sit in a half-empty high school auditorium to hear your nephew play the guitar and sing "Hang Down Your Head, Tom Dooley." And to make plans to take your goddaughter to Paris for her sixteenth birthday—just the two of you—to visit the catacombs and go ice-skating under the Eiffel Tower.

Staying in touch with the adults in your family may require that you be the accommodating sibling rather than the alpha female. You may find that it is very restful to put aside your ego for the sake of the group. Try to practice giving up control the next time you have an opportunity to attend an Elvis-themed birthday celebration in Las Vegas for a third cousin you hardly know. Don't you sometimes have the sneaky feeling that your family was invented solely to test your sense of humor?

> Only with relatives can you savor the sweet
> and sour absurdities of life.

While you are collecting mileage points—family reunions are the fastest-growing segment in the travel industry—you are also extending your network of contacts a billionfold.

Indeed, family interconnectedness resembles the interconnectedness of the cells in our brain, whose complex, three-dimensional information architecture allows each of its 100 billion neurons to be within only four steps of each other. Likewise, you and I, because of our relatives, the relatives of our relatives, and their relatives' relatives, are never more than four degrees of separation from any of the 6 billion people on the planet.

So never again apologize for your relatives. Make time in

your life for your aunt Millie, your nephew Charles, and even your sister's obnoxious twins and her nerdy husband. Each of them is the gateway to a hundred thousand people whose names you'll never know but who are nonetheless your distant cousins.

Among them are a schoolteacher in Cameroon, a Zen master who emigrated from Korea to the south of France, a Los Angeles police officer, the captain of a tugboat in New York Harbor, a medical student in Ceylon, and the adorable five-year-old girl who lives next door.

· ·

life

(THE ART OF BEING LUCKY)

THERE are two kinds of luck, and you want both. The first has to do with what you have (a great house, a darling husband, a good job), while the second has to do with what you don't have (a terminal illness, a lawsuit, a sick child).

The first kind of luck can be described as the pursuit of happiness, while the second kind is a fountainhead where, at all times, one can instantly experience pure joy.

As we all wait for those swell fifteen minutes of fame that are supposedly coming our way, why not try to experience luck in the present tense?

Why not say right now, "I am lucky," instead of waiting for fortune to smile on us in order to say "I was lucky" in the past tense?

Indeed, the first kind of luck only happens in hindsight, in the rearview mirror of our mind, as a redemption mechanism that gives sense to everything that happened before, while the second kind of luck is immediate, convenient, and democratic to boot.

No special status is necessary to be ecstatic upon learning that you don't have cancer after all or that you don't owe the government any back taxes.

But if you are proactive about it, you can feel just as lucky as someone who recently received some long-awaited good news, without having to endure a period of debilitating anxiety beforehand.

You can feel lucky right now for not being born in a country where women have no legal rights, for instance. You can also feel lucky for small favors, like for not having inherited your father's bad temper, or for not feeling threatened when you meet people who are smarter or wealthier than you are.

Feeling lucky for not being someone else is the ultimate achievement.

People with a major disability are often endowed with a form of courage that is nothing short of amazing. They profess to feel lucky for being alive, even though they lack the opportunities the rest of us take for granted.

Let this be a lesson.

To feel lucky all the time, maybe all we need to do is to view our most comfortable assumptions as a disability. We are disabled indeed when we assume that being famous would be an advantage, for instance. Or that success can be measured by the appreciation of others. Or that we must be deserving in order to be lucky.

If you don't confuse luck with meritocracy, you will never have to pretend that you are better than you are. To the *New York Times* journalist who will call you when, at long last, you become famous (as you surely will), you will explain that your success was really accidental. During the phone interview, you will cheerfully downplay your personal achievements. As proof that your good fortune is pure chance, you will proudly flaunt your past shortcomings—your bad haircuts, weird boyfriends, lousy school grades, recurring weight problem, and even your tendency to drive too fast.

Ultimately, that is what fame will give you: not public recognition, but the right to joyfully claim who you are—the right to say, "I am lucky not to be someone I am not."

In America, we believe that our happiness depends on getting breaks, even though being American is already the biggest break we will ever get.

That said, you and I cannot take advantage of our lucky situation on the planet unless we question the popular notion that luck equals success, and that fortune is synonymous with fame.

Being lucky, for instance, protects you, while being successful reinforces your sense of vulnerability. Even if your name brings up 149,000 entries on Google, you still might find yourself sitting on the edge of the bathtub one morning wondering whether your life makes sense.

Even if you have a lot of money in the bank, when you draw cash from the ATM machine, you will notice the tendons, blue veins, and wrinkles on the back of your hands.

And even if you travel only in first class, you will still feel left behind when you see a flock of geese heading south in the open sky.

Success is a modern invention whose main effect is to make the most self-confident among us feel very lonely at times.

In the stretch limousine that will take you to the taping of *Oprah*—that day you will be her only featured guest—you will be on the phone with your son's fourth-grade teacher discussing your little boy's disruptive conduct in class. And when, a month later, you find yourself sitting next to Jodie Foster at a charity luncheon, you will be mortified to realize that you are the only woman at the table who did not get a manicure for the occasion.

If you are so lucky as to be happy, maybe you should avoid becoming successful.

Happiness and *happening* have the same root, the old Norse word *happ*, which meant good luck or "happy accident." For the fierce Vikings, the word *happiness* was not synonymous with contentment but with prosperity and success. Only later did the three concepts of happiness, luck, and success evolve to mean three different things.

Still, today, in the popular imagination, the confusion endures. We can't help but assume that lucky breaks are conducive to happiness. We ignore cautionary tales about lottery winners whose personal lives were ruined by their wealth, or tabloid accounts of glamorous people destroyed by the effects fame had on their egos.

So, naturally, you and I rejoice the day our significant other gets a big promotion, but we are unprepared for the consequences. We are hurt—and genuinely surprised—when a week later he uncharacteristically snaps at us because we forgot to pick up his shirts from the dry cleaner.

For better or for worse, for richer, for poorer . . . when we tie the knot, we vow to stand by each other, bracing ourselves as we imagine the worse—unaware that we should instead brace ourselves for the better.

When trying to strike a happy balance
between life and work, success is the biggest
stumbling block.

Success could tear you apart. He has to clean up the cat box when you are away on a media tour. He brings you flowers for your birthday, but the next day you buy yourself a diamond ring. Your twice-weekly sessions with your personal trainer cost more than his Tuesday visits to his therapist.

Or maybe it's the other way around. He expects you to supervise the remodeling of the bedroom walk-in closet that has to be enlarged to accommodate his extensive collection of three-piece suits. He calls you from Hong Kong in the middle of the night to ask you to cancel his dentist appointment. He falls asleep while you describe to him the conversation you had with Isaac Mizrahi, whom you met at a book-signing party.

Last but not least, you no longer like the same movies.

It makes you nostalgic for the days when happiness meant sharing the same umbrella, using bowls for lack of plates, and taking public transportation to City Hall instead of hiring a white stretch limo.

You felt lucky back then, when what you didn't have did not spoil the delight you felt when you were together, even though you were so broke you couldn't afford extra cheese on your pizza and slept in a secondhand sofa bed in a third-floor walk-up.

You cannot control what you will get from life,
but you can learn to be lucky all the same.

Only when you reject clichés about
success will you be so lucky
as to be very fortunate in the end.

Given a chance to write the perfect scenario of a lucky life, one in which you get everything you want, chances are you could never come up with a satisfactory yarn.

Scriptwriters often describe how they rarely know the specifics of a plotline before they write it. Even though they may have an outline, the final result rarely resembles the original synopsis. Their best scripts happen when they allow their fictional characters to improvise as they go along.

Likewise, you cannot control what you will get from life, but you can learn to be lucky all the same. The trick is to get so organized that eventually something in your program will go astray and Lady Luck will have no choice but to show her hand.

The best strategy is to treat your life as a journey, happiness as an adventure, and "having it all" as a daring expedition to find the Land of Oz.

When learning to be lucky, traveling
is the metaphor of choice.

Book your life choices in advance the same way you would book flights, car rentals, hotels, and excursions. Figure out early on in your career whether you intend to be financially independent or marry a rich man, join the ranks of the professional elite or be the stay-at-home type, postpone having children or find part-time employment. Then fasten your seat belt and sit tight as you watch your trajectory veer off course.

It is not a bad idea to go abroad before setting out on a life path in order to experience firsthand what happens when a failure to follow the best-laid plans turns an ordinary vacation into a life-changing adventure.

The night before an outing in Rio, Barcelona, Istanbul, or Florence, make a point of carefully perusing the map to locate the various monuments you want to visit. Study the subway system and alternate bus routes. Write down the hours of the guided tours and the exact addresses of the museums and the restaurants recommended by friends.

Being prepared gives you the extra confidence you will need to take calculated risks: linger too long over lunch, let yourself be seduced by a roadside attraction, try a shortcut and insist that you are not lost even though you have been wandering for forty minutes in a neighborhood where people dry their laundry on clotheslines stretched across narrow streets.

It is usually then that luck smiles on you. The tipping point is likely to be a weird coincidence. Quite by chance, in a small chapel, you come across a lesser-known fresco by Piero della Francesca, which, amazingly, happens to be one of your absolute favorite quattrocento paintings. Or you discover around the bend a Mallet-Stevens apartment house, the same one that was on the cover of the in-flight magazine you read on the plane coming over.

When randomness gets up close and personal, you know that you are on the right track.

Luck is a premonition. Though you don't
know what will happen next, you feel that
you have secured the blessings of the gods.

On a trip, extricate yourself from the maze of tourist destinations; only then will you have a chance to stumble across the authentic little Art Nouveau bistro where, five years hence, you will return with your boyfriend and he will propose to you.

In life, only when you take the chance of being a little wrong will things turn out to be right when all is said and done.

• •